your *from Birth to 18 Months* Baby

Nancy Stewart

FISHER
er
BOOKS™

To Shawn, Leighton, Josie and Ben,
with thanks for joining us

Commissioning Editor: **Sian Facer**
Art Director: **Jacqui Small**
Executive Art Editor: **Keith Martin**
Art Editor: **Lisa Tai**
Editor: **Jane MacIntosh**
Cover and Special
   Photography: **Sandra Lousada**
Stylist: **Sheila Birkenshaw**
Illustrator: **Dawn Gunby**
Picture Researcher: **Wendy Gay**
Production Controller: **Nicola Connell**
North American
   Editors: **Margaret Martin and Sarah Trotta**
Cover design: **FifthStreetdesign**
North American
   Publishers: **Bill Fisher, Howard W. Fisher, Helen V. Fisher**

Published by:

Fisher Books
4239 W. Ina Road, Suite 101
Tucson, AZ 84741
(520) 744-6110

ISBN 1-66651-134-6

The author has asserted her moral rights.
All rights reserved.

First published in Great Britain in 1995 under the title:
PRACTICAL PARENTING: *Your Baby from Birth to 18 Months* by Hamlyn, an imprint of Reed International Books, Limited, Michelin House, 81 Fulham Road, London SW3 6RB

© 1995 Reed Books Limited

Printed in Hong Kong
Printing 5 4 3 2 1

Library of Congress Cataloging-in-Publication Data

Stewart, Nancy, 1951—
   Your baby : from birth to 18 months / Nancy Stewart.
      p.   cm.
   Includes index.
   ISBN 1-55561-134-6
   1. Infants (Newborn)—Care.   2. Infants—Care.
      3. Infants—
   Development.   I. Title.
RJ253.S74   1997
649´.122—dc21   97-8170
                                                   CIP

Picture Credits

Cover Photograph: Sandra Lousada

Angela Hampton—Family Life Pictures: 6, 36, 39, 82, 99, 104, 106, 111, 112, 113, 118, 129, 143, 146, 156, 160, 163, 167, 175

Bubbles—Jacqui Farrow 182, Geoff du Feu 177, Julie Fisher 140, S. Price 151, Loisjoy Thurston 61, 69, 139, Ian West 78, 92, Jennie Woodcock 116

Child Growth Foundation: 124 © 1995 Child Growth Foundation; growth charts reproduced with the kind permission of the Child Growth Foundation, 2 Mayfield Avenue, London W4 IPW.

Collections: Sandra Lousada 10, 87, 123, 130, 164, Anthea Sieveking 4, 7, 27, 52, 91, 132, 170

Sally and Richard Greenhill 42, 64

Image Bank: Jeff Hunter 76, F. St. C. Renard 125

Sandra Lousada 2, 8/9, 20/21, 48/49, 66/67, 81, 84/85, 96/97, 108/109, 120, 136/137, 149, 153, 158/159, 166, 169, 172/173

Lupe Cunha 89, 115

Reflections Photo Library: Jennie Woodcock 13, 14, 51, 75, 101, 126, 127, 155, 183 right

Tony Stone Images: Bruce Ayres 6/7, 12, Christopher Bissell 13, Ken Fisher 11, Rosanne Olson 103, Terry Vine 5

The publishers would like to thank the parents and babies who kindly modeled for this book.

Contents

Introduction

The first 18 months with your baby are a journey of discovery. You find new feelings within yourself and develop new skills and knowledge. Most of all, you watch the character emerge of the new and unique person who has come to share your life. It's a time of wonder. You may see the world with new eyes as you watch your baby grow and change. You will see your baby begin to make sense of the world, develop bonds of love and learn to communicate.

Being a parent is a huge and responsible job. New parents need information about their role. This book brings together information and thoughts to provide a guide about all the parts of your baby's life. It provides up-to-date information about babies, their health and development, and family life. The book is meant to bring support to new parents. It provides useful tips from other parents' experiences. And it should help build confidence in being a parent.

You do need good information about how to do things. But in many ways your best teacher is your baby. Each baby is a unique person. What suits your baby and you may be different from everyone else. This book provides a framework of facts about all babies. It offers advice based on the experience of other parents. With this book, your own experience and your own baby's reactions, you will develop your own style as a parent.

Having a baby connects you in a new way with the vast human experience of one generation giving life to the next. I would like to thank all the parents who have shared their experiences with me. I am grateful, too, to *Practical Parenting* editor Helen Gill for her guidance and vision both in my contributions to the magazine and in writing this book. My greatest thanks is of course to my four children, who continue to be my teachers, and to my husband John, who is with me every step of the way.

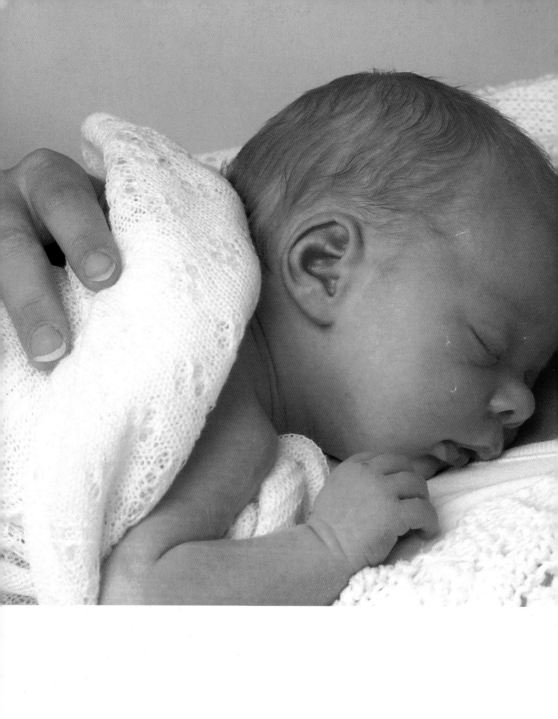

1

Meeting Your Baby

So there he was—this calm little baby with squashed ears. He seemed like a stranger instead of the baby I'd been living with for nine months. He looked really old. Dan said he looked like his grandfather. Over the next few days and weeks, he seemed to grow younger and younger. The wrinkles disappeared and his skin got soft and rosy.

BECOMING A PARENT

Giving birth is a momentous experience. Whatever sort of labor you have had, it has marked an enormous change in your life. A minute before, you were pregnant. Then suddenly you hold in your arms a new person who breathes, cries, squirms, watches and listens.

You have both just taken your first step along the road of being parent and child. Your whole job as a parent could be summed up as helping your child become independent. Through your love, support and teaching, your child will one day become able to manage on his own. The tall order for your baby is to grow up, from needing you for everything to becoming a fully independent adult.

Birth marks huge progress on this long journey. For the past months, your baby has needed you to breathe for him, eat for him, keep him warm and protect him inside your own body. But now he is ready to begin taking on some of these things for himself.

TIME TOGETHER

You and your baby already knew each other before birth. He has heard your heartbeat day and night. He listened to your voice and felt the rhythms of your daily life. You have felt his kicks and wiggles, maybe even his hiccups. You also know his quiet, sleepy times. Fathers, too, may have been jabbed by a little knee or foot. Your baby may know the father's voice, which drifted into his world.

After the upheaval of birth, everything shifted. Is this the knee you watched rolling under your skin last night? Is this the weight you carried these past weeks? Now your baby has a face and a sex. Your baby is now one real person instead of all the thoughts you imagined before.

For your baby, it's all a new world. Air floods into his lungs. His skin is shocked by cold air and then by strange textures. Lights and sounds are so much more intense than those he has known before. Instead of the steady pressure crowding and cradling him in the womb, there is space all around him. He feels uneven pressures as he is lifted and held.

You both need time to absorb what has happened, and to get to know each other. The time right after birth is a time of heightened emotions and awareness. You will want to look over, feel and marvel at your baby. You will begin to absorb the fact that the birth is over. You are now a mother in a different sense. Quiet, private time together for parents and their baby is an important last stage of the birth.

" My first reaction was, 'Who is this? She's finally here!' I was so anxious to meet my child. It's like you've known a person by phone or writing and then you see their face for the first time. There's that special look, like she knows you. " PATTY

Your first moments with your baby will stay with you forever, even as she changes and grows. Holding this complete little person in your arms for the first time brings feelings you can never anticipate.

Your baby, of course, doesn't understand what has happened. He doesn't even know that he is one person and you are another. But in the midst of all that is new for him, he will know your heartbeat and breathing. He will know your voice, and the feeling of being warm and held closely. You will comfort him as you hold him in your arms and talk to him.

FIRST IMPRESSIONS

You may be surprised as you check over your newborn. A new baby looks quite different from the rosy-cheeked older babies you see on baby products and greeting cards. At birth, she shows signs of having just come from the watery world of the womb. She will be wet and slippery. She may be streaked with blood. Being born puts your baby under pressure and stress. She may also show some effects of the birth process itself.

Head

A baby's head is large for her body. At birth, the head may be pushed into a long shape. The forehead may seem short, or the head may be lopsided. This is caused by *molding*, which allows the large head to change shape to come through the narrow birth passage safely. The effect lasts only a few hours. Your baby's head quickly becomes more rounded and even.

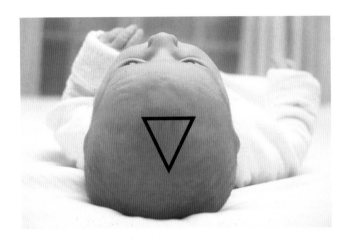

You might notice your baby's pulse beating in the larger fontanel shown by the triangle. You may see it bulge slightly when she cries. If you ever notice the fontanel bulging a lot, or sunk down, this can be a sign of illness. Report this to your doctor right away.

A baby's skull is not solid. Instead, it is formed of plates of soft bone joined by fibrous tissue. There are six soft spots, or *fontanels*. These are the gaps between the bones of the head. You may only notice the two main ones. The largest is a diamond-shaped spot about 1-1/2 inches (4cm) across, at the top of the head. Behind that you might see a smaller, triangular soft spot. These soft spots will close up between the ages of nine and 18 months.

There may be swellings on your baby's head that don't go away quickly. A large, firm swelling of the skin caused by pressure during birth is called a *caput*. This may take a few days to disappear. Or there may be an egg-shaped lump on one side of the head. This bruise on the outside of the skull is called a *cephalhematoma*. It may take a few weeks to flatten out. It does no harm and will go away without treatment.

If your baby was delivered by forceps, she may have minor bruising or shallow dents on the sides of her head. Vacuum extraction may have left a swelling or red mark where the suction cup was applied. These marks often go away within a few days.

Arms and Legs

A newborn's arms and legs may seem small next to her large head and abdomen. But you will be delighted by her perfect little hands and feet. A baby born at full term will have fingernails that reach to the ends of her fingers. Her legs will be slightly bowed. Her feet will be turned in from having been curled up inside the womb.

Color

At first, your baby's hands and feet may look pale or bluish while her body is pink. This is because her blood is not yet being sent very strongly to all of her body. It may also cause uneven color in her body. The top half may be pale and the bottom half red. Changing her position can help to sort it out.

Hair

Some babies are born with a thick crop of hair. Others are almost bald. The color of your baby's hair may not last. It's common for the first hair to fall out in the early weeks. When new hair grows, it may be another color.

There may also be fine body hair, called *lanugo*. This is often found over the ears, shoulders and down the back. All babies have lanugo in the womb. Babies born early are likely to have some still present at birth. It rubs off in a few days.

Skin

Your baby's skin will be covered with *vernix*, a creamy whitish substance. Vernix protected her skin from the waters of the womb. It can be thick over much of the face and body. Or it can be slight and show up mostly in the folds under the arms or elsewhere. Vernix will protect your baby's delicate skin in the first few days. It's better not to wash it off. Let it be absorbed by the skin.

Tiny white raised spots over your baby's face are called *milia*. These are swollen or blocked sweat and oil glands in the skin. These may be caused by the hormones from the placenta. They are normal and will go away soon, so don't squeeze them.

Dry or peeling skin at birth, often on the hands and feet, is not a sign of eczema or other skin problems. Dry skin should settle down after a few days.

Birthmarks

Many babies have small, flat red marks on the skin. You find these most often on the eyelids, forehead and back of the neck. These marks are caused by enlarged blood vessels. They often vanish within the first year. Bluish blotches may be found on the lower back. They are most common on

Skin-to-skin contact gives pleasure and comfort to both you and your baby. It is an important part of getting to know each other. Nothing speaks better than the language of touch, as you hold and stroke your baby.

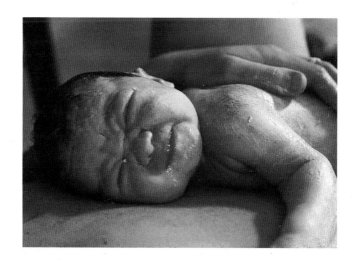

dark-skinned babies. They are caused by uneven skin pigment. These marks are harmless and will fade.

A strawberry mark may be present at birth. Or one may appear after a few days. It may be raised, red and soft. Such marks will grow bigger over a few months. But be patient. It will fade and then vanish without treatment.

Eyes

Your baby's eyelids may be puffy from the pressure of birth. This swelling will go down in a day or two. There may be small spots of blood in the white of the eye, from tiny burst blood vessels. This will also soon go. Almost all newborns' eyes are bluish-gray. The pigment in the iris hasn't developed yet. It can be months before your baby's true eye color appears. But some brown-eyed babies will have brown eyes from birth.

When your baby cries, you won't see any tears. The tear glands only start making tears after a few weeks.

Mouth

Your baby's tongue may be attached to the bottom of her mouth along most of its length. This won't affect her sucking and is no cause for worry. As the tongue grows, it grows mainly from the tip.

There may be tiny pale spots inside the mouth, along the gums and on the roof of the mouth. They are small cysts. These, too, will vanish without treatment.

Breasts and genitals

Both boys and girls react to the mother's hormones during pregnancy. Breasts may be swollen. A few drops of milk may even appear. This swelling will go away in a few days, as the mother's hormones clear out of the baby's system.

Genitals may also be enlarged. In girl babies, there may be a clear or white discharge. There may even be a few drops of blood from the vagina as a result of the hormones. This, too, will stop by itself in a couple of days.

BONDING

How soon can you expect your excitement at seeing your new baby to become love? "Bonding" is what we call the process of becoming so devoted to your baby that you are happy to take on all the duties of being a parent for the months and years that follow. Human babies need more care for a longer time than any other creature. The strong instinctive love of parents for their baby has a purpose. It is the reason you give up

" At first I was relieved to know that the baby was healthy and everything was fine. They took him to do the Apgar test. So I didn't hold him for about two minutes. But the second I held him, that was it— such joy. " SHARON

14

your own sleep. It's why you take care of your baby's every need. And it's why you put your own wishes second as long as your child needs you.

Early contact

The time right after birth can be a special stage in falling in love with your baby. For both parents, the stress of labor gives way to a new life. The miracle of birth opens the way to strong feelings. Your baby, too, will be more open to meeting you in the hour or two after being born.

"An hour or so later my wife Peggy went to have a shower. One of the nurses said, 'I'll take her and put her in a crib now.' She really insisted. I said, 'No, she's staying with me. She's my daughter.' I think if she had tried to take her I'd have flattened her there and then. I'd talked to other fathers. But nothing prepared me for the powerful burst of emotions I'd feel. All of a sudden this helpless little baby was all ours." ANDREW

For one thing, both mother and baby receive hormones involved in labor and birth. *Endorphins* are one group of chemicals from the brain. These are the body's own painkillers. They help you relax and feel better. At birth, both mother and baby can have high levels of endorphins. This may account for the "high" many mothers feel after giving birth. It may also be the reason that babies, if they have not received drugs used in labor, are likely to be calm and very aware right after birth. After this alert time, a baby will fall into a deep sleep. There may not be such a long, quiet, aware time again for a few days.

Right after birth, the mother also begins to produce *prolactin*. This is the hormone that makes milk. Prolactin also causes you to feel calm and relaxed. This hormone is sometimes called the *mothering hormone*. It may help you bond with your baby.

So the time right after birth is an ideal time for you to meet your baby. It may be love at first sight. Many women feel a great surge of love for their baby as they first hold her in their arms, feel her soft warmth, speak to her and see her quiet gaze.

The memory of this time may stay with you all your life. But this is only one starting point for loving your baby. Some women feel in touch with their babies during pregnancy and already love them before birth. Many other women have little feeling for the baby at first. It is often two or three days before a mother feels love for her baby. And it's not rare for it to be up to two weeks.

Love needs to grow

There are many reasons for not having much feeling for your baby as soon as she is born. You may feel tired and drained by labor. You may not have the energy to respond to your baby. You may feel mostly relief that the birth is over. You might just want to rest. The type of birth can affect your feelings. If it was long and hard, you may feel upset. If many drugs were used, you may feel groggy, and your baby may be sleepy or cranky. Other issues in your life

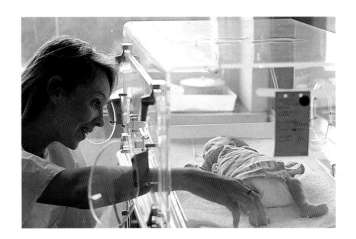

If your baby is in an incubator, at first you may be able only to stroke and talk to him. But just being there and helping in his care as much as you can will ease your worries. You can help him progress in a way nobody else can.

can cloud your feelings. Problems with your partner or other children, money worries or not feeling certain about this pregnancy can affect the way you feel. Or it could just be that women react in different ways. Some mothers feel a slower growth of that special bond.

There is no need to worry or feel you are not a good a mother if you don't feel love right away. Bonding does not just happen. It is a growing feeling that develops as you and your baby get to know each other. For mothers who miss out on early contact, if mother or baby was ill or for those who have adopted babies, the love that grows will be just as strong as for those who got off to a quicker start.

You need privacy and enough time together to help love grow. You need time away from other people and other problems. You need to watch your baby, talk to him and have a lot of close contact. Babies are fun to hold, with their big eyes, soft warm body and scent that arouses your maternal instincts. Love is a two-way street. Your baby will be playing his part by watching you. He will want to look into your eyes. Within days, he will respond to your voice and your smell and be comforted by you.

Sometimes, a mother with postpartum depression will keep on having dulled feelings for her baby. If after two weeks you still don't feel much for your baby, tell your healthcare provider. He or she can make sure you receive the help you may need for depression.

SPECIAL CARE

Most babies born at full term are strong and well. But sometimes a baby needs special medical care from birth. Babies who weigh under 5-1/2 pounds (2.5kg) are called *low birth weight*. They may need help and special care in the first few days. Some babies are small just because their parents are small. Such babies are fully mature and don't need extra help. But most small babies are either premature or small-for-date. Premature babies are born too soon. Some body systems may not yet be ready to function well. Small-for-date babies are of low weight for their age. Not enough nourishment reached the baby through the placenta.

Both small-for-date and premature babies may have trouble holding their body heat. They have low sugar reserves. So they must be fed often and blood-sugar levels must be checked. Premature babies may have breathing problems. Such babies need to be in an incubator with extra oxygen and warmth.

Sometimes you may be able to keep your baby's incubator beside your bed. But a baby who is ill or needs extra care, will need to stay in an intensive-care nursery. There the expert staff can keep a close eye on your baby and provide care as needed.

Parents' reactions

It can come as quite a shock if your baby needs special care at birth and can't be with you. If your baby is born early, you may not feel ready. You will also feel anxious about your baby's condition. You might even feel guilty because you cannot look after him by yourself. Strong feelings like these, or even anger at the staff, your partner or the baby, are common when your baby is having problems.

When you see your tiny, helpless baby attached to high-tech equipment, with wires and IVs and expert staff, you may feel out of place and useless. But your role in helping your baby is still important. Medical staff will want you to spend as much time with your baby as you can. Your presence, your touch and your voice will give comfort and strength to your baby.

If you go home from the hospital before your baby, you may want very much to stay with your baby in the hospital. Get any help you can from relatives or friends. When your baby is stronger, you will be able to hold and feed him. When it's time to take him home, lots of cuddling and holding will build your confidence and help make up for his shaky start.

MALFORMATIONS

When a baby is born with a physical malformation, the first reaction is often shock or disbelief. Anger, guilt and sadness may follow quickly.

You need good information to limit worry as much as possible. You also need the facts about the baby's prospects and possible treatment. Will an operation be necessary? If so, when? With the shock of the discovery, parents may not understand what they are told. You will need repeated chances to ask questions and to learn all you can. Along with medical staff, there may be a counselor at the hospital to help parents. There are also special support and information groups for the more common malformations, such as cleft palate or Down syndrome (see Appendix).

The fact that the baby is not perfect can overwhelm you at first. But the baby as a person will soon shine through. As parents come to terms with the problem, they can love their baby for the unique, special person he is.

POSTPARTUM TIPS

◆ *When you hold your newborn, remember that she may look fragile, but she is in fact very sturdy. She won't break. When you hold her without tension, she can relax, too, and feel secure.*

◆ *She needs you to support her head in holding or lifting her. Her neck muscles aren't yet strong enough to take the weight of the head.*

◆ *As long as all is well, your time together after birth doesn't have to be cut short for routines. Ask the staff to wait until you are ready before they weigh and measure your baby. She can also be checked right in your arms.*

◆ *Try putting your baby to the breast in the hour or so right after birth. She may not nurse at first. If she doesn't, try again. Getting started soon after birth is a good boost to successful breast-feeding.*

◆ *Take some photos of your first meeting with your baby. She will change almost from moment to moment in the first few days. You'll value the reminders.*

◆ *Even if you are tired after the birth, you may be too excited to sleep. Having your baby with you to cuddle, or to see peacefully sleeping, will help you absorb what has happened.*

QUESTIONS AND ANSWERS

Q: My baby's breathing isn't regular. He breathes very fast for a while. Then sometimes it seems he's hardly breathing at all. Is there something wrong with him?

A: It is normal for a young baby to shift between panting, fast breaths and shallow breathing. He will be about three months old before it settles down into a more steady rhythm. A newborn baby breathes about twice as fast as an adult. He may also make snuffling sounds because his air passages are so small. Or he may have hiccups, which can look scary because they shake his whole chest. But hiccups don't bother him at all.

Q: Is it all right for a baby to be delivered to the mother's tummy and cuddled right away? Or does the baby need to be wrapped up first?

A: A new baby loses heat easily, so you need to keep him warm. The baby could be dried and wrapped to maintain body heat. But skin-to-skin contact with the mother will also keep the baby warm. If the baby is held against the mother and covered with a warm cloth, the mother's body heat will keep the baby warm. Both mother and baby will enjoy the body contact. Babies lose the most heat through their head. If you drape a cloth around the head, you can keep the baby from cooling too much.

Q: My baby smiled in her sleep when she was just two hours old. Was this really smiling, or just a chance movement?

A: Some people would say it wasn't a "real" smile, because it wasn't a smile done on purpose in response to something. It will be some weeks before your baby smiles at you on purpose. But early smiles like your daughter's seem to come when the baby feels peaceful and relaxed. Such smiles may be signs of pleasure or just feeling good.

Q: Because my baby's hands and feet are a little blue because of his circulation, how can I tell if he's cold?

A: You can check his body heat by feeling his back or tummy. If they feel about the same as your own, he is all right. Don't worry about hands and feet being a little blue or pale in the first few days. But if the lips or tongue look blue, tell your doctor or healthcare provider.

Q: I put my baby to the breast soon after birth and he sucked well right away. But I know there won't be any real milk yet. He's a big baby. Will he be hungry before my milk comes in?

A: Although true breast milk isn't produced right at birth, when your baby sucks he does receive *colostrum*. This "pre-milk" is rich in proteins. It is also full of immune factors that protect your baby from disease. Even though there may be only small amounts of it, it will sustain your baby very well until your milk comes in. Because it has less fat than true milk, colostrum is easier for your baby to digest. Keep putting your baby to the breast so he can get plenty of colostrum. His sucking will help the milk to come in.

2

The First Week

❝ The first few days felt like magic. I wanted to slow them down to hold on to them forever. She still seemed only half real. She didn't seem to be in the same world as the rest of us because she was changing so fast. I could sit for hours, just watching her face. ❞

BASIC NEEDS

As soon as your baby is born, you have to provide for all her needs. In many ways, life was simpler when you were still pregnant. You didn't have to think about feeding her and dealing with her wastes. Your body kept her warm and protected, with a cozy place to sleep. After giving birth, you may have thought you had a lot more to do! But in fact your baby's basic needs are still very simple. As long as they are met, she will not be very fussy about the details.

So take your time over the first few days to settle in and learn together. Get to know what your baby can do and what she responds to. You may be amazed by how quickly she learns. With her first instinctive suck, the first feeding can seem to happen almost by accident. Soon she will calm down at the sound of your voice. She will get ready for the feeding she has learned to expect as you hold her in position. She will be using all her senses to learn about this world. But best of all, she will learn that it is a safe place where she will be cared for and loved.

Warmth

A new baby has little body fat to keep him warm. He can't react to changes in temperature as fast as an adult, to maintain his body heat. The room

Early checkups by healthcare staff will follow your baby's progress. Checkups include basic functions such as breathing and maintaining body heat, and weight and physical condition. If you have any worries your healthcare provider will be glad to talk them over with you. He or she will explain the usual progress over the first few days.

temperature should be warm, around 70F (21C) for the first few days. The baby should also be kept out of drafts. Your body makes a perfect heater, so your baby will be cozy and warm snuggled in with you.

Food

Hunger is new for your baby. The need to be fed is so important that he feels it as an urgent pain if food doesn't come right away. When he is hungry, he will cry loudly. He will become frantic if he isn't fed quickly. You don't have to wait for him to get very upset, though. He will almost always wake up hungry. If you nurse him when he wakes and stirs, he won't have to become upset in order for food to arrive. He will then go smoothly from being asleep to being awake and full. And he will be learning to trust life and you. Don't worry about changing your baby until after he is fed. Most young babies fill their diapers as a reflex during a feeding. So you would have to change him again afterward, anyway. There is no point delaying the feeding and having him get upset while you change him.

Sleep

Most new babies sleep a lot, between 16 and 20 hours a day. Day and night may have no meaning for your baby. He may be most wakeful and active at night, which is tiring for you. You can teach him that nights are for sleeping by keeping things dark and quiet for the nighttime feedings. In the daytime, don't worry about keeping things quiet. Sudden loud noises will startle and may wake your baby. But he is used to a lot of steady rumbling and thumping noises in the womb. He won't be bothered by noise. It will be easier as he grows older, too, if he gets used to sleeping through household noises.

Physical contact

Touching, being held, is another of your baby's basic needs. He has gone from the full contact of the womb to the scary emptiness of space. He feels more secure in your arms. Movement and feeling the rhythm of your breathing and heartbeat also comfort him. As you hold him, be sure you are relaxed yourself. If you feel tense and awkward in a position, he will too. As long as you support his head, and he feels securely but gently held, he will relax.

When you go to pick him up, talk to him and touch him to let him know you are there. Then he won't be startled by sudden movement. With one hand, raise his feet enough for you to slide the other hand under his head, to support his back and head. With one hand under his back and head, and the other under his bottom, pick him up. And keep talking to him. When you put him down, keep your hands under his head and bottom as you lay him down. Then slide them out. (See page 24 for ways to hold and handle your newborn baby.)

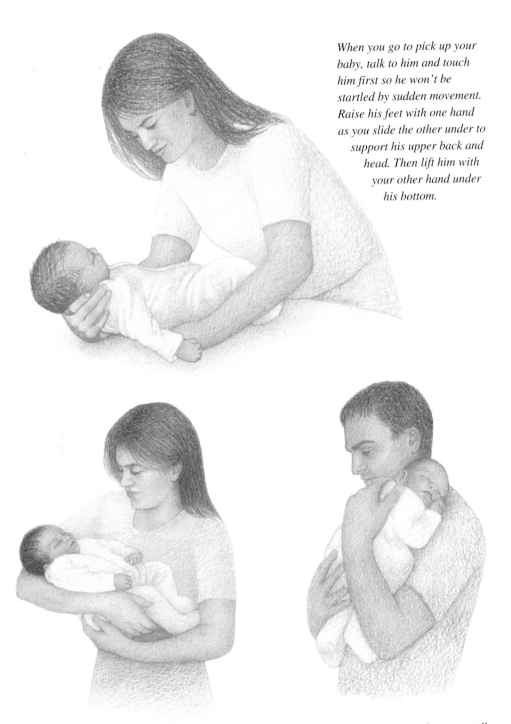

When you go to pick up your baby, talk to him and touch him first so he won't be startled by sudden movement. Raise his feet with one hand as you slide the other under to support his upper back and head. Then lift him with your other hand under his bottom.

Your baby's head is supported and she feels secure when cradled in your arms.

A baby enjoys your movement when you walk around with his head resting on your shoulder.

24

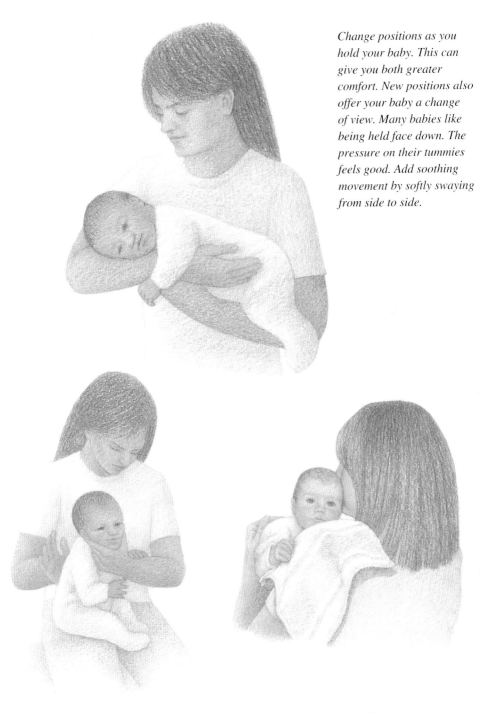

Change positions as you hold your baby. This can give you both greater comfort. New positions also offer your baby a change of view. Many babies like being held face down. The pressure on their tummies feels good. Add soothing movement by softly swaying from side to side.

Help your baby to bring up gas by rubbing her back as you hold her on your lap.

You can also hold your baby against your shoulder to burp her.

REFLEXES

At first, much of your baby's movement is by reflex. Reflexes happen by instinct in response to stimulation. Some basic reflexes are vital to life, such as the breathing reflex, emptying of bladder and bowel and the hunger reflex that makes her demand food. As she grows, more of her actions will come under her control instead of being a reflex.

You might notice other reflexes such as blinking and closing her eyes against bright light, or pulling away from pain. Some reflexes in a newborn baby do not last long.

Sucking reflex: Your baby will suck when something is placed in her mouth. She may even have practiced in the womb by sucking her thumb. A good sucking reflex helps get feeding started. In premature babies, the sucking reflex may be delayed. Tube feeding may be required at first.

Rooting reflex: If you brush something against your baby's cheek, she will turn her head to that side and open her mouth. This is called the *rooting reflex*. It helps her to find the nipple (see page 55).

Grasp reflex: Your newborn baby will grip your finger if you touch his palm (see pages 20 and 21). His grasp is so tight that he can support his whole body if you lift with one of your fingers in each of his hands. This reflex may come from early times when a baby needed to cling to his mother. The soles of his feet also curl up when stroked. This reflex goes away in a few months. Then he has to learn to grasp things on purpose.

Startle reflex: If your baby is startled by a loud noise or sudden movement, she will react with her whole body. This is the *startle* or *Moro reflex*. She will fling out her arms and legs as if to grab something. She will also throw her head back, open her eyes wide and maybe even cry (see illustration on opposite page).

Crawling reflex: If you place your newborn on her front, she will find a crawling position. Her legs are still tucked towards her body as they were in the womb.

Walking and stepping reflexes: If you hold your baby upright so her feet touch a hard surface, you will see the walking reflex. She will move her legs as if walking forward. If her shin touches something, she will raise her leg as if to step over it. This walking reflex will soon be gone. It is not the same as walking on purpose, which she will master many months later.

SENSING THE WORLD

Your baby is highly aware. While you are watching him and learning all you can about him, he is taking in the world around him. The part of his world that attracts him most is you. His interest in you is his part of the bonding process. This helps the two of you to communicate.

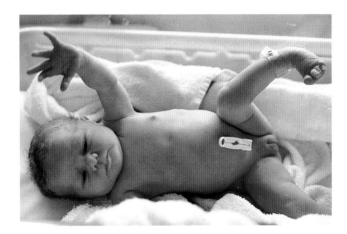

Much of your baby's early movement is by reflex, such as the startle reflex in response to sudden loud noise or movement. The arms and legs fling out wide, as if to catch something. Eyes open wide, and the baby may cry.

Sight

A newborn baby can see quite well. He has a clear focus on objects about 10 inches (25cm) away. Farther away things look more blurry. When you hold your baby in your arms and he looks at you intently, he sees you clearly. New babies prefer to look at a human face over any other shape. They focus most on the eyes. Eye contact is one of the main ways people communicate. When your baby seeks out your gaze, it helps you feel connected to him. In only 36 hours after birth, your baby can recognize the shape and outline of your face. He will prefer to look at your face rather than at others. He will also follow you with his eyes as you move.

Babies see colors and patterns. They seem to prefer curved lines to straight ones, objects to flat pictures, colors to black and white and complex rather than simple patterns.

Hearing

Most babies hear well. Even before birth, your baby listened to your voice as well as to many other noises. Because he knows your voice, he will respond with greater interest when you speak. By the third day of life, a baby will turn to the sound of his own mother calling his name rather than other voices.

Most mothers use a more high-pitched, soft, cooing voice when speaking to their babies. In fact, this is the voice range a new baby hears best and prefers. Your baby also responds to human speech. He will subtly move his body in rhythm to the speech.

Taste and smell

Most babies can taste and smell quite well. Your baby prefers sweet tastes, such as breast milk. By one week of age, he can tell the taste and smell of your milk from the milk of other mothers. He likes the milky smell, which helps

27

him settle down to nurse. He is also attracted to his mother's body smell. He will turn away from unpleasant odors, though.

Touch

The skin and awareness of touch are the first sense organs your baby developed. He learns about the world around him through all the new sensations of temperature, pressure and texture. As you handle your baby—stroking, swaying, rocking or cuddling—you are getting to know each other in a unique way. Touch is in some ways the most direct communication between people.

MINOR WORRIES

Newborn babies may get a number of minor ailments. These can worry parents if they are not prepared for them. Here are some of the most common ones.

Navel

When the umbilical cord has finished its job at birth, it is often clamped about 1 inch (2.5cm) from the baby's belly and then cut. After about 48 hours, the cord stump has shrunk and the clamp can be removed. During the first week after birth, the stump continues to shrivel. Bacteria soften the base so the cord finally drops off. This can happen any time from four days to six weeks later, leaving the navel.

The cord should be kept clean and dry. Gentle washing with warm water twice a day is fine. Antiseptic cleaners will just slow down the process of the cord dropping off. You can gently pull on the stump to clean in the gutter around the base. After the first day, a tiny bit of bleeding from around the stump is not a problem. But if the place around the stump looks red, there could be an infection, so tell your doctor or healthcare provider.

Vomiting mucus

A lot of mucus may be produced by your baby's stomach after the birth. She may vomit it up in the first day or two. It may be bloodstained. And your baby may nurse less at that time. It can also get in the way of her breathing for a moment. But she has a strong cough reflex and will clear it out of the way. Just lay her on her side if she needs to cough it up.

" A funny thing happened when I went into the hospital to see them the morning after the birth. I walked into the ward and heard my baby cry. I knew it was her right away. I didn't even have to ask the nurse. I knew her cry right away. And I'd only been with her for maybe three hours the night before. " KEITH

Sticky Eyes

Many babies develop a discharge from one or both eyes in the days after the birth. This may cause the eye to run or have sticky matter in it. The lids may even be stuck shut after sleep.

Your doctor should have a look at the eye. But it is not often an eye infection (conjunctivitis) that could be passed on to the other eye or to someone else. Instead, it is often just a blocked tear duct.

The tear ducts are tiny tubes that run from the corner of the eyes. They collect the tears, which are always being made to keep the eye moist. Then they pass them down into the nose cavity. In small babies, there can be a blockage at the bottom end of the tear duct. This creates a moist site where germs can grow, causing the discharge. A blocked tear duct needs no treatment. It will almost always clear up by itself. If a baby still has a blocked tear duct at six months, treatment by an eye doctor might be needed.

To clean the eye, use a piece of soft cotton cloth dipped in cooled boiled water. Wipe from the outer edge of the eye into the inner corner. Use a clean piece of cotton cloth for each eye. Your doctor may prescribe some antibiotic drops. These will not cure the problem. But they may reduce the stickiness while the body clears the blockage.

"I just loved the first weeks when he was a tiny, tiny baby. He was so vulnerable and dependent. In some ways, although I know it's not quite true, I thought, 'I'm the only one who can do it.' I felt so proud and thought, 'Gosh, he's so pretty!' I think all mothers think their babies are pretty. **"** MELANIE

Squint
A lack of muscle power to control the eyes may make your baby seem to squint. You might notice this when she is relaxed and nursing. As her muscles develop, she should be able to focus both eyes together by about three months.

Sniffles
A young baby may sound sniffly in her breathing. This is the result of small air passages rattling with extra mucus. The nose makes mucus to protect the delicate nasal lining from milk, which may get into her nose in the early days. It doesn't mean your baby has a cold. If she did, she would also have a fever or seem ill in other ways.

Rashes
Skin is not just a barrier as we sometimes think. It is a living organ that absorbs many substances. Rashes in the early days may be harmless signs of the skin reacting to its new world. Your baby's skin may react to its first contact with clothing or other substances with a red, blotchy rash that has a white or yellow center. They may come and go quickly on different parts of the body. Such a rash will clear up after a couple of days and needs no treatment.

Your baby may get a heat rash in hot weather or if she is too warmly dressed in any weather. A heat rash has tiny red spots that spread where the baby perspires. It shows up most often on the face, neck, shoulders and chest, and in skin folds. Rinse off the sweat to soothe the skin. Make sure you do not dress your baby too warmly. And don't use too many blankets when she's sleeping.

Dry skin

Most babies have dry, peeling skin a few days after birth. The top layer of skin, which was in contact with the amniotic fluid, will be shed. It needs no treatment. But you could rub on a little good-quality oil, such as almond or olive.

Pink-stained diapers

A pink stain in the diaper may be urate crystals from the baby's urine and is normal. With a girl, there could be a little blood from the vagina. This can be caused by the mother's hormones and will stop in a few days.

Jaundice

Many newborns develop a yellow tinge to the skin and in the whites of the eyes on day two or three. This is known as *normal newborn jaundice*. It is a result of the baby's liver not being able to process and get rid of bilirubin. *Bilirubin* is made when red blood cells break down. This goes on all the time in the body as red blood cells reach the end of their life span. It can happen a little more often in the first few days because your baby needed more red

LOOKING AFTER YOUR NEWBORN

- *Try making faces at your baby. From the very first day, she will watch you. She will copy you if you stick out your tongue a few times.*
- *Nights will be less tiring for you if you keep your baby in bed with you, or right beside your bed.*
- *Change your baby after a feeding, not before. Then she won't have to wait and get upset. She will likely need changing afterward anyway. When she's older and can wait to nurse, you can change her first.*
- *Some babies feel more secure and sleep better if they are swaddled, wrapped snugly in a cloth or shawl (see page 91).*
- *Whatever sort of diapers you decide to use later, newborn-size disposables are handy for the first few days.*
- *Talk to your baby. It doesn't matter what you say. Don't feel silly if you find yourself using a high-pitched "babytalk" voice. It will be just right for your baby, and she will love it.*

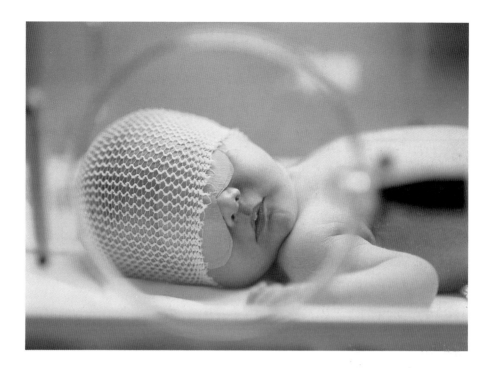

blood cells to carry oxygen before birth than he does now that he is breathing for himself. The liver doesn't excrete the bilirubin well. So it can build up in the bloodstream, making the yellow color. The bilirubin level often peaks at about day four or five. If the baby remains alert and nurses well, nothing needs to be done. If the bilirubin were to reach very high amounts, though, it could damage the baby's brain. Your healthcare profes-sional will keep an eye on your baby's color. He or she may arrange a blood test if there are signs of jaundice. Treatment would be started long before damage could begin. The treatment is called *phototherapy*. It involves expos-ing the naked baby, with pads to protect his eyes, to ultraviolet light.

It can be upsetting not to hold your baby except to nurse. But phototherapy can often be given beside your bed so you can still touch and talk to your baby.

MEDICAL CARE

As soon as your baby was born, he was given a quick check to see that he breathes well and there are no major problems. At one minute after birth, and again at five minutes, an Apgar score will be taken. This measures how well he is handling the transition to life outside the womb. The Apgar score is a quick assessment method that gives up to two points each for heartrate, breathing, muscle tone, body color and reflex response.

Physical exam

Later, when you and your baby have rested, a doctor will give him a more complete exam. If your baby was born in a hospital, this exam will be made by a pediatrician. It will be repeated when you are ready to leave the hospital. If your baby was born at home or at a birthing center, your family doctor or other healthcare provider will perform the exam.

The doctor will observe your baby. She or he will measure his head and check the fontanelles, eyes and mouth. She or he will also check the abdomen and listen to the baby's heart and breathing.

Your baby's hips will be looked at to check the joints. Many babies have "clicky hips" because the ligaments are loose. This can result from pregnancy hormones the baby was exposed to in the womb. But a few babies have an extra-shallow hip socket (congenital dislocation of the hip). If not treated, this can lead to a permanent limp and trouble walking.

The doctor will also check the baby's genitals. With boys, she or he will see whether both testes are in the scrotum. The testes are formed in the abdomen. They come down into the scrotum before birth. But sometimes one or both has not yet descended. They can also go up and down at first. If the testes are not in the scrotum, the doctor will make a note to keep an eye on the situation.

During the first week, a nurse will take a drop of blood by pricking your baby's heel for the PKU test. The blood sample is checked for very rare genetic conditions in which the baby cannot break down some nutrients or use them properly in the body. Other tests may also be done on the blood sample to detect thyroid problems or cystic fibrosis.

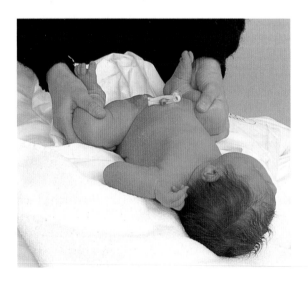

All babies are checked for congenital dislocation of the hip. If discovered before the age of six months, an affected baby can be fitted with a harness. The harness holds up the hips at right angles to the body. This keeps the baby from stretching out her legs. After about 12 weeks, the harness can be removed. A deep hip socket will have formed and the hip joint will be normal.

QUESTIONS AND ANSWERS

Q: My baby weighed just over 8 pounds when she was born. The midwife said she would probably lose some weight at first. Why is that?

A: Most babies do lose some of their birth weight before starting to gain weight again. Losing about half a pound (227g) or even as much as one-tenth of the birth weight is common. Most of this loss is fluid. In the first day or so, your baby may not nurse much, but her urine output stays normal. And it may be two or three days before your milk comes in. But not all babies lose weight. If yours is born hungry and nurses a lot in the first 24 hours, your milk may come in sooner and she may not lose weight.

Q: Even after a feeding, my baby keeps making sucking movements with his mouth. He seems restless and doesn't settle down to sleep. Should I give him a pacifier?

A: Starting to rely on a pacifier right away isn't a good idea. If you are breast-feeding, the time your baby spends sucking on the pacifier might be better spent at the breast to get breast-feeding going. A baby sucks for comfort as well as for food. There is no harm in letting him have a longer time at the breast even when you think he is not hungry. It may help him settle down to sleep. Or you could try holding or swaddling him (see page 91) when he is restless.

Q: My baby's cord has fallen off. But there is a bulge under the navel that comes out more when he cries. Is something wrong?

A: The swelling is an umbilical hernia. This is fairly common in babies and not a problem. The gap in the muscle wall of the abdomen where the cord came through has not closed fully. The contents of the abdomen push through when pressure is raised by crying or coughing. It is not painful for your baby. Nothing needs to be done. Almost all umbilical hernias close by themselves before age five.

Q: Will a baby be spoiled if you pick her up when she cries?

A: It's not possible to spoil a new baby. In fact, babies whose mothers go right to them, instead of leaving them to cry, soon cry less and are easier to comfort (see pages 98-99). She's crying because something is wrong, not because she wants to control you. If you can solve the problem, whether it's hunger, a dirty diaper or loneliness, she will calm down. She will also learn that she can trust you and that the two of you are partners.

Q: Why are newborn babies given Vitamin K?

A: Soon after birth, you will be offered Vitamin K for your baby. It is given as a shot or in liquid drops. This vitamin helps blood to clot and is often given routinely. It may be more important for preterm babies or babies who have had a difficult birth. But discuss it with your doctor if you have any questions.

3

Getting
Settled

*" I was amazed how much time it took
just to look after him. All day long I
just seemed to be chasing my tail. I
couldn't get anything done except the
most basic things. Then I'd look at him
lying there peacefully asleep. I'd wonder
how such a tiny creature could have
such an impact, running two adults
around in circles. "*

EARLY DAYS

The birth of your baby and the first few days bring an excitement that sets them apart. But before long, you enter a new phase as you settle in at home. This involves weaving your new baby into your daily life. Your days (and nights) will never be quite the same again. Your days must now be organized around your baby's needs. There are also emotional adjustments for everyone concerned.

When babies are born at home, settling into a rhythm after the first few days may be simpler. You can keep up the pattern you have established since the birth. The sights, sounds and smells of home become familiar to your baby. Though you have had doctors or midwives visiting, you have been on your own quite a bit. You have set up your own way of doing things from the start.

When you bring your baby home from the hospita, you will have an extra adjustment to make. Instead of having help and advice from the hospital staff, you will be on your own. You may be anxious and have doubts about how you will manage. You will also have to get your own meals and manage a household. Your baby, too, will react to the change.

Take plenty of time to rest and just be with your baby. This helps smooth the way in the transition to daily life.

The change to regular life needs time and care. Don't try to rush too soon into the wider world. Keep

your focus on yourself and your baby. It's best if both parents can be home together for a week or two after the birth. Then both father and mother have a chance to tune in to the baby and learn together. It takes time to build confidence with basic handling, bathing, diaper changing and so on.

> **"** *I loved people coming in and giving me a lot of attention. It's a celebration. It can be a bit too much if people stay hours and hours. But it's nice because you can tell your story over and over. You get advice from people and can ask questions. I was on cloud nine.* **"** PATTY

Above all, a new mother needs rest. Her partner can help by taking care of meals, shopping, housework and looking after any other children. This is also a time for a couple to learn their new roles as parents.

Friends and relatives may be eager to come and admire the baby. But be careful not to wear yourself out with too many guests. You may love being the center of so much attention. But you may also regret it later when you are exhausted with a crying baby in the middle of the night. The best guests are those who offer to make you a cup of coffee instead of expecting you to wait on them. Good visitors will also keep a visit short. If someone shows up when you are about to take a nap, or stays too long, speak up! Explain that you are tired and need to rest.

It may help to have a relative stay for the first few days at home. But be sure it is someone who is there to help out, not to make more work for you. It's best if a helper sees her role as keeping things running smoothly around you. You and your partner need plenty of time to be with your baby.

BECOMING A MOTHER

Becoming a mother is bound to affect you profoundly. Your feelings may range from joy to grief. You may feel pride and delight in your baby or resentment at the amount of work and lack of sleep. You may feel excitement or frustration and boredom. And it's common to be confused by feeling conflicting emotions at the same time.

"Baby blues"

A few days after giving birth or within the first week or so at home, you may be hit by a let-down feeling. You may be delighted with your baby. But you may still find yourself crying for no reason you can put your finger on. You might get upset with those around you. Down feelings after giving birth are known as the *baby blues*. These feelings may be linked to the rapid hormone changes that follow childbirth. Tiredness is also a factor. You may also feel let down after all the waiting of pregnancy and the excitement of your baby's birth. Many new mothers even feel a bit left out. It can seem like everyone cares about the baby, while mother isn't very important anymore. If you do have a day (or a few) where you feel down and tears seem to arrive from nowhere, it helps to know that baby blues are common and don't last long.

But don't put all your feelings down to baby blues as if that will explain them away. Becoming a mother involves a huge change in your life and your view of yourself, which makes it a truly demanding time. Even changes in life you are happy about require adjustments. It's not always an easy process.

New role as mother

Some things are lost when you become a mother. They may be replaced by other things you'll enjoy. But that doesn't mean you won't have some doubts or fears about letting them go. One thing you have to let go of is your view of yourself as a child-free woman. Instead, you need to take on an image as a mother. "Mother" means different things to different people. You might have to tell yourself that you can still be young, sexy and smart. You still need to value yourself as a person, not just as a mother. So before long it will be important to make sure you have time for your own interests and fun.

If you have given up an outside job to have your baby, you might have a loss of income as well as missing the satisfaction of your work. Our culture rewards a job with money and the approval that comes from having done a job well. Although you are working very hard as a mother, our culture gives mothers low status. There is no one there to list your duties and say "nice going" when you have achieved something. So it's no wonder that confidence and self-esteem can droop.

You may also miss your social contacts, both through work and with friends who don't have children. It's no longer so easy to decide on the spur of the moment to go out. And you may be too tired when friends are free at night. Your social life is sure to change. But you can cut down the problem of loneliness if you make the effort. Your baby is more portable in the early months before he starts solid food than he will be later. So do get out with him. Try to see friends at noon if you need to get to bed early.

You may lose touch with some people from your pre-child days. But your child will also help you make new friends for years to come. Contact someone you met at childbirth classes or at your doctor's office. There may be a mother-baby group nearby. Check with your local La Leche League, YWCA, or with a church or temple near you.

Adjusting to "child time" can be hard also. You can no longer plan your day and stick to it. You don't know when you will be working and when you will have free time. You are now on 24-hour call and you can't predict from one day to the next just when you will be needed. You end up trying to do a few things at once. You never finish many of them. It's natural

" We don't have grandparents nearby, and felt really alone. That's where La Leche League came in. It was great to get in touch with other people with babies. " HEATHER

It may seem hard to get out with your baby, but it's worth the effort. No one likes to feel lonely and isolated. Other mothers are a good source of friendship and support as you share your new experiences.

that you will sometimes feel frustrated and distracted. It doesn't help to try to stick to a routine, because your baby doesn't read the clock. Slowly life *will* fall into more of a rhythm. But it is never fixed because your baby's needs will change as he grows and develops. The key is to be flexible. You may even find that you enjoy a pace of life that responds to present needs. And you may feel good about the way you can keep several things in your mind at once.

Don't expect too much of yourself. Sometimes a woman who gives up work to stay home with a baby feels she must prove herself by being "super-woman." No one can keep a perfect house, make great meals and deal with every aspect of life with a baby. Instead, accept any help offered. And take your time. You will learn to be more organized and efficient.

Let your household standards drop. Focus on yourself and your baby. As long as the main things are done, it doesn't really matter if there is dust on a shelf or the dishes are still in the sink. Most of us have certain jobs that need to be done before we can relax. Other tasks can be put off until later. Work out which are most important to you and do the very least you can feel happy with.

Your health

All the demands of new motherhood are easier to manage if you are feeling well yourself. Don't neglect to eat well. Good nutrition will help you recover from pregnancy and birth more quickly. The right foods will also give you the energy you need. If you are breast-feeding, you are still providing your baby's nutrition, too. You may not have time for cooking, or feel much like eating proper meals. So stock up on healthful foods that are easy to prepare and that you can enjoy through the day.

It's scary to come home from the hospital. There were hundreds of people there to tell you what to do and when. And then you get home and think, 'Now what do I do?' We thought we should always be doing something with her. But after a while we learned that she'll just get by with things on her own. When she needs something, she'll let us know. ALICIA

Now is not the time to think about dieting to lose weight. Even if you are not breast-feeding, good nutrition is more important than a slim figure at this point in your life. Any weight loss should be slow, over several months.

Exercise is the best way for you to affect your shape. Exercise is also good for your sense of well-being. Even if you feel too tired to bother, try some gentle, regular exercise. You'll find it gives you more energy and makes you feel better.

Your need for rest is enormous. At least once during the day, lie down and rest or sleep. If you have other small children, you could have a quiet nap time with them. Resist the urge to get something done when your baby sleeps, or while someone else looks after him. Instead, use the time to rest.

The postpartum checkup at about six weeks will give you a chance to seek advice or help with any problems. But don't wait until then, nor think it is the last word, if you have lasting pain from the birth. For some women, painful stitches can be a problem months later. Back pain is also common. Don't think it is something you have to put up with. Seek help. Be persistent, if you have to. And get a second opinion.

Postpartum depression

Sometimes the baby blues don't fade away quickly, but linger and grow worse. Or a mother who has been feeling well may become depressed months after the birth. If you have signs of depression for more than a week or two, any time in the first year after your baby is born, it can be serious. Postpartum depression can last for many months if it isn't recognized and treated. Depression doesn't just mean feeling blue. It can appear as tiredness and feeling ill. You might feel hopeless, or have unexplained aches and pains. You might have trouble sleeping or feel anxious, tense and grouchy. Or you might feel confused and find it hard to concentrate.

Postpartum depression is often hidden. You may disguise it, because you think that you should be feeling happy. Other people might not know how bad you feel, because you may cheer up when you see them. Postpartum depression does, in fact, affect one or two out of every ten new mothers. It will pass in time. Simply knowing that can help. But real help in other ways can also be important.

If you think you might be depressed, talk over how you feel with your partner, family or a friend. Their extra care and understanding, as well as practical help, can give you a real boost. Get plenty of rest. Depression is worse when you are tired. Talk things over with your doctor. You might want to take your partner or a friend with you. It will help them to understand postpartum depression and enable them to be more supportive. Sometimes medication can ease the symptoms of depression until things settle down. With help, you can begin to enjoy your life and new baby more fully.

BECOMING A FATHER

Fatherhood can bring great joy. It also brings a sense of responsibility. Many fathers are very close to their partners and involved in the changes of pregnancy. But you cannot be as closely aware of your baby as his mother, who carries him. At birth, seeing this new person who has sprung from you and your partner can make you feel both proud and humble.

There can be a down side, though. A new father faces many of the same issues as a new mother. You, too, have to deal with loss of sleep, less social life, less money and a new self-image as a father. If you have taken on the role of family breadwinner, you may feel under pressure from increased financial demands.

Some fathers find it hard to adjust to a family of three. In the early weeks much of the baby care may be handled by the mother. This can leave a man

TIPS FOR GETTING SETTLED

- *Get plenty of rest. Unplug the phone when you lie down for a nap.*
- *Do any jobs you have to do early in the day. You'll have more energy then than you will have later.*
- *Carry your baby in a sling that gives good head support. This will soothe her and leave your hands free to get things done.*
- *Keep a supply of changing things in the living room as well as the bedroom. This helps cut down on trips through the house.*
- *Make lists for shopping so you can be efficient while you're out. Or let someone else do it for you.*
- *Make double batches of meals. Use one now and freeze one for later. Make casseroles early in the day and reheat them later.*
- *Talk to other mothers at the doctor's office or when you're shopping so you don't feel lonely. A baby is a good ice-breaker.*
- *Don't hover over your partner while he changes or dresses your baby. He needs a chance to practice so he can feel competent.*
- *Take some time for yourself. Go shopping or exercise. A new outfit or hairstyle might give you a boost.*

Left: A father's role in baby care may vary. It can range from helping now and then to being the primary caregiver while the mother works outside the home. Getting the right balance is not always easy. That's why you need to discuss your plans for childcare.

Below right: Everything shifts when a baby comes along. New facets are added to your relationship with your partner. No matter how much you enjoy your baby, though, a couple still needs time for each other.

feeling like a spare part. You may feel jealous of the closeness between mother and baby. And you may miss the time spent together and the closeness you shared with your partner before the baby arrived.

Get involved with your baby right from the start. Then you are much less likely to feel left out. You will feel competent as a parent and part of the new family when you take an active role from the early days. If your baby is breast-fed, you will be left out of the nursing relationship. You may give a bottle from time to time. But your role in supporting your partner so she can breast-feed is vital. Many fathers take delight in the peaceful sight of the mother breast-feeding their baby.

You need to do your part in sharing baby care to allow the mother to rest. You also have to build your own relationship with your baby. You might enjoy bathing your baby, massaging, holding and talking to him, or going for a walk with your baby in a sling.

BEING A COUPLE

Becoming parents adds a new dimension to your relationship. You now share a lifelong commitment as parents to your child. At the same time, all the work of looking after a baby and the emotional ups and downs can sometimes keep you apart.

Talk over how you feel so you can each help support the other. This will bring you closer and help release pressure from any stress or strains between you. Show each other understanding. Give practical help, too. Each of you needs a break sometimes. And try to make sure you have some time together as a couple. You need to be able to enjoy each other apart from being parents.

Sex

There is no right time to resume lovemaking after your baby is born. Some women feel ready and have interest in sex before their postpartum checkup. But for some couples it will be much longer. Tiredness often gets in the way. A woman who has been cuddling and touching her baby all day may also want some space to herself in the evening. Some couples need time to see each other as sexual partners again, instead of "mother" and "father." A woman may not feel good about her body after pregnancy and may not feel attractive. She may need sensitive wooing.

Differences in readiness for sex can cause tensions. But try to be very patient and talk over how you feel. Remember that your relationship is not just about sex. You can show you care and enjoy each other in other ways.

Soreness from stitches can delay the return of sexual relations. There are lots of ways besides full penetration to enjoy sex together. Try new things and find what feels good to you. After you give birth and sometimes while you are breast-feeding, the vagina may not produce much lubrication. This can make sex uncomfortable. Try using a vaginal lubricant from a pharmacy. Be very slow and gentle with penetration. If soreness or pain persists, there may be a problem with your stitches healing. See your gynecologist if you don't feel better.

THE LARGER FAMILY

If you already have children, a new baby in the family will also affect them. By the age of five, a child will often take a new baby more or less in her stride. But a 2- or 3-year-old may feel left out and very jealous. After all, she has had you to herself all her life. It's very hard to find that now she must wait for her story and has much less time with you. After the excitement wears off, she may decide it's time the troublesome baby disappeared!

She may become clingy or act like a baby herself. She may wet her bed, want to be fed—or make a fuss to try to get your attention. It can be hard to be patient when she acts like this. But she really needs to know that you still love her. Even with a very young child, it sometimes helps to talk about the negative feelings. Talk about how having a baby can be a nuisance in some ways. This will help her know that you understand and still love her even though she has these feelings.

Try to find times when she can have your full attention. A father can have a special role here in doing things with an older child while the mother is with the baby or rests. But a child needs time with her mother, too. It helps if she can see there are some benefits to being an older child. Give her some treats or special privileges that come from being a "big girl." Let her help you take care of the baby. Give her small jobs to do, such as handing you things or smoothing lotion on the baby's feet. This can help her feel part of what's going on and that the baby isn't just yours but belongs to all of you as a family.

Grandparents, too, will welcome the new baby. You may understand your parents better as you learn what they went through when you were a baby. Grandparents may be willing helpers and can be a great source of support and advice. Practices may have changed since they were young parents. But they may also have a greater perspective on things. Ask for advice if you want it. But be clear that you are the adult in charge of your baby. Let them know you will make the final decisions about what is right for you and your family.

SHARING CARE

You and your baby will come to learn each other's signals. You will establish your own unique language. You may feel that no one else could possibly look after your baby. In the first few days and weeks after birth, you may almost have an invisible umbilical cord that keeps you tied to your baby. Your baby's attachment to you is central and unique. But there is no need to exclude other people from caring for your baby.

There are several reasons why you may need to share the care of your baby with someone else. You may want a night out with your partner. You may need some time for yourself to follow your own interests. Or you might need to work away from home.

At first, you may share baby care with your partner. It is useful to talk over your roles. Is childcare mainly your job, with your partner helping out now and then? Or are you truly planning to share the tasks of parenthood? In many families, the father takes on some daily routines, such as bathtime or playing with an older baby. The mother often provides the rest of the baby's care. Some couples, though, share all aspects of being parents more evenly. Then each partner can have some time to him- or herself. And the baby is left in competent hands.

A new baby is exciting for an older child, but it can be a mixed blessing. Sharing parents' attention may not be easy. And a small baby isn't much fun to play with. The older child needs to know she is valued. She also needs to have you to herself sometimes.

A friend or relative may agree to look after your baby. You may pay a babysitter. Or you may swap childcare with other parents. Whoever will be in charge, be sure to tell them your baby's routines and any special needs. Even with young babies, it's best if the caregiver is someone your baby knows. This becomes even more important when your baby is a few months old and begins to react to strangers.

" I have to focus on different things now that I'm not at work. If I found a job it would be hard to organize things for someone to look after Anna. I don't want to give that up. I'm lucky I don't have to work. I'd rather have a couple of years with her completely, with all the ups and downs. " SHARON

Back to work

You may have mixed feelings if you are going back to work. You may feel guilty about leaving your baby. You may be concerned about good childcare. And you will miss being with her. On the other hand, you may need to keep your hand in at work. You may need to be earning money or you may thrive best in your job.

Keep in mind that if you do enjoy your work, you may be more refreshed when you are with your baby. Her shorter time with you may be better than spending all day together if you are frustrated and bored at home.

As long as the childcare you arrange provides consistent, loving care, your baby will be fine. You and your partner may decide it suits you best for him to take on the childcare role at home while you go out to work. Or a relative may step in to look after the baby, often a grandmother.

Other choices include a nanny or group care in a day-care center. There are good and bad sides to each. But base your choice on your own gut feeling about the quality of care. Is there real caring for your child? Is it easy for you to speak with the caregiver? Do you understand each other?

Things will be easier if your baby already knows the caregiver before being left with her. Even if you plan to go back to work when your baby is a few months old, it's good to begin childcare early. Try to spend some time with your baby and the caregiver before you go back to work.

If you are working, don't overload yourself. Don't expect to come home and do most of the housework. It may not be enough for your partner to take the baby for a walk while you do the cooking. You may want to divide the housework as well. You both will need to juggle your many tasks. Talk over how to share all that needs to be done. This will give you the best chance of meeting your own needs and those you share as a family.

QUESTIONS AND ANSWERS

Q: I feel nervous about caring for my baby. There are so many things I don't know. I might get something important wrong. And people give me different advice, so who should I believe?

A: There is no end to the different views on childcare. None of them are all right or all wrong. Different things work for different parents and babies. Only you can find out what suits you and your baby best. Listen to advice. But then trust your own instincts and believe your own experience. Don't be afraid of trial and error. Serious mistakes are rare if you use basic common sense. And babies are tougher than you may think. No parent ever gets it all right. But we do the best we can. And that's good enough for happy, healthy children.

Q: I'm a single parent. It's really hard to manage everything. Do you have any suggestions?

A: Being on your own with a baby can mean extra pressures due to lack of money, loneliness and the amount of work. Look for help from anyone who can lend a hand and give you a break. You could contact single-parent organizations such as the National Organization of Single Mothers (see Appendix) to see if there is a single-parents' support group near you. Or perhaps you could start one. You'll find moral support in talking things over with other single parents. You might also exchange childcare to give each other some free time. In the United States, contact the Women's Bureau Clearinghouse (see Appendix) about state laws on family leave. Contact your own health insurance company to learn about benefits for you and your child. If your income is low and you have no health insurance, contact your state or county Health Department. You may qualify for Medicaid insurance for your baby. You may also find good support from WIC, the supplemental feeding program for mothers with low income and their babies. In Canada, contact your provinicial or territorial Ministry of Health (see Appendix) to learn about health benefits and programs.

Q: I expected to have a lot of time when my baby would sleep during the day or be contented. But instead he's awake most of the day and has to be carried or held all the time. Isn't this unusual?

A: It's hard when life with your baby isn't what you expected. Parents who have a firm idea of what to expect can find it harder to cope than those who just take it as it comes. Every baby is different. While some are calm, others are more demanding and need to be held and comforted more. The amount of sleep a young baby needs varies a lot, too. Try not to think about an average baby or an ideal baby. Just focus on your baby as a person and what he needs.

Q: If I leave my baby with my mother, could he get attached to her instead of me?

A: A baby doesn't have to make just one bond. He can be attached to two or more people. Often the closest bond is to the mother. But the baby can also be attached to others who will do when the mother isn't there. It's nice if your baby does become attached to your mother. That means he is being well cared for. As long as you are there for important times like bedtime, and your son knows he can trust your love, your mother won't be taking your place in his eyes.

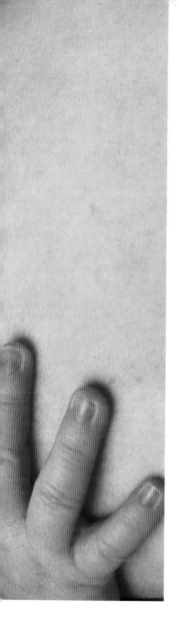

4

Feeding
Your Baby

" It never crossed my mind to use a bottle. Breast-feeding is so much easier. It's always there. It's always ready. And I think it's better. Some of my friends don't really like to do it. They breast-feed because they think they should. But I think it's nicer. It's natural, and she seems to like it. "

MORE THAN JUST NOURISHMENT

Besides providing nourishment for growth, feeding your baby also provides a time of special closeness. For your baby, it brings the bliss of a satisfied stomach. She is held in your arms and able to watch your face and play with you. For you it is a peaceful lull. It is a pleasure to have your baby snuggled against you. You hear her swallows, first eager and then contented. And you see her stop to smile at you or drift into sleep.

There is no question that breast milk is the ideal food for babies. Your child will do best if nothing else is given for the first four to six months of life. Breast milk is better than formula milk, both for your baby's health and for you. But if you choose to bottle-feed, or end up using a bottle because of feeding problems, your baby will still thrive. The closeness of feeding times can still be important for both you and your baby.

BREAST-FEEDING

Breast milk is the perfect food. It is designed by nature to suit human babies. It is such a complex and changing substance that even the best formula milks cannot copy it exactly.

What's so good about breast milk?

Ideal food: It contains the ideal amounts and types of protein, fats, sugars, vitamins and minerals. It also contains immune factors, hormones and enzymes that help to make it easy for your baby to digest. Not all the substances in breast milk are fully known. More are discovered all the time. Breast milk can't be copied.

Breast milk changes as your baby grows to meet your baby's changing needs. The very first milk, *colostrum,* is ideal for a newborn. It is rich in immune factors, fat and protein. It also helps to clear the baby's bowel and gives it a protective lining. Breast milk itself varies when produced for a premature baby, a young baby or an older baby. It also changes within a feeding. The first milk satisfies your baby's thirst. Then richer milk satisfies her hunger. This gives your baby more control over how much nourishment she will take. Breast milk also helps keep her from becoming overweight as a baby and later in life.

Protection from illness: Breast-fed babies are far less likely to suffer from stomach upsets and diarrhea. Breast milk is always sterile and free from bacteria. It also contains substances that coat the walls of a baby's intestines. These prevent germs from being absorbed.

Infectious illnesses are also much less likely because of the immune factors in breast milk. During pregnancy, your baby was protected by your antibodies. After a few weeks, she will slowly begin to make her own. Breast-feeding fills the gap for a young baby. Breast milk contains antibodies and white blood cells that fight infection.

Protection from allergies: Allergies such as eczema, asthma and hay fever are less likely in a breast-fed baby. If they do turn up, they tend to appear later and be less severe. This effect is linked to the protective coating of the gut. It also helps if you don't feed your baby cow's-milk proteins, which may trigger allergies. If there are allergies in your family, exclusive breast-feeding for the first six months or more is the best way to protect your baby from developing allergies.

The only problems I had breast-feeding were that I was very sore. And I had too much milk. I had to get up in the night and change the bed for weeks because I leaked so much. When I nursed on one side, I had to hold a towel to the other breast to catch the flow. JUDITH

It costs nothing: Breast milk is free. There is no need to buy feeding and sterilizing equipment or formula milk. Breast-feeding saves quite a bit of time and money over a few months.

It's easy: Breast milk is always ready. It's sterile and at just the right temperature. You don't have to wash, sterilize, mix or heat. It's much easier to take your baby anywhere. And night feedings are much less tiring. You can feed your baby in bed so you hardly need to wake up.

Good for you: Breast-feeding releases hormones that help your uterus shrink back to normal more quickly. You need good nutrition and should not diet to lose weight while breast-feeding. Even so, many breast-feeding mothers find they lose weight more quickly because of the calories burned up in making milk. Breast-feeding may also protect you against cancer of the breast, ovaries and cervix later in life.

Breast-feeding is easy. It is a great help for busy parents. There is no work preparing formula. There's nothing to carry when you go out. And the milk is always ready. It's sterile and the right temperature even for nursing your baby on the beach, like this mother.

A pleasant time: Many mothers love the feeling of nursing their babies. They enjoy providing for their baby as they did before birth. The skin-to-skin contact provides a special closeness that may help with bonding. The hormone *prolactin*, which triggers milk production, also helps you feel relaxed.

Your baby likes to nurse for the comfort and pleasure it gives her, as well as for food. She shouldn't be allowed to bottle-feed just for comfort. She could become obese from overfeeding. But even when the breast is nearly empty, she can still nurse for the comfort it provides.

How milk is made

During pregnancy, your hormones cause cells that make milk to develop in your breasts. By late pregnancy, they begin to produce small amounts of colostrum. After the birth, there is a sudden rise in the hormone prolactin. This brings about the first true milk. But from then on, it is nursing your baby that causes the milk to be made. It is a perfect system of supply and demand. The more your baby nurses, the more milk is made. This means there will always be the right amount for your baby's needs.

When your baby nurses on the breast, a message goes from the nerves in your nipple to your brain. It tells your system that the baby needs milk and how much. The pituitary gland in your brain responds. It releases two hormones, prolactin, which causes the milk to be made, and oxytocin, which helps release the milk in the breast for your baby.

To express milk, support your breast with one hand. With the other hand, place your thumb and fingers on opposite sides, well behind the nipple. First press back toward your chest wall. Then bring your thumb and fingers together, and roll forward slightly. Continue this motion. And be patient. It may take a while to get it right. Put a warm washcloth on your breast before expressing. It may help the milk to flow. Rotate the position of your hand to empty different parts of the breast.

The milk is produced in cells called *alveoli*. Each is surrounded by muscle cells that can contract to squeeze the milk down ducts toward the nipple. Before reaching the nipple, the ducts widen. There is a reservoir for milk just behind the nipple (see page 55).

Your baby doesn't really suck on the nipple. She takes it pretty far back in her mouth and keeps it there. Her jaws open and close on the part around the nipple, the areola. This forces the milk stored in the reservoirs out through the openings in the nipple. Your baby receives this first "foremilk" of the feeding. Foremilk has less fat than the later milk but is more thirst-quenching.

When I went back to work I rented an electric breast pump so I could express milk to leave for Jessamine. It worked well although sometimes I felt like a cow on a milking machine. She always refused to take a bottle from me when she knew she could have the breast. But she would accept a bottle from my husband. **HEATHER**

In response to her sucking, oxytocin is released. It causes the muscles around the alveoli to contract. This sends the richer milk streaming down from where it is produced right to your baby. This is called the *letdown reflex*. You may feel it as a tingling far back in the breast. Once the letdown has occurred, your baby doesn't have to suck very much. The rich hindmilk comes in a steady trickle or even a spurting stream. She only needs a little suction to anchor the nipple in her mouth while she swallows the milk.

Getting started

It's best if you breast-feed your baby sometime in the first hour or so after birth, while your baby is alert. A good start at this time can help both you and your baby. It helps you set a pattern that can continue whenever you nurse. Some babies, though, don't want to nurse soon after birth. Or you may not be able to put the baby to the breast right away if you have had an anesthetic or your baby needs special care. In that case, take time as soon as you can to have the first feeding and get things started.

A calm, private room can help you and your baby relax and learn together. A lactation consultant can guide you if you feel uncertain. Later you may find it easy and restful to nurse your baby lying down. But it is easier for the first feeding to be sitting up. You can put a pillow on your lap to support your arm holding your baby. That way you won't have to lean forward and strain your back.

Your baby's position is as important as yours. Hold him with his neck in the crook of your elbow. Your forearm will support his body. His back should be straight, with his head slightly higher than his body. He should be free to turn his head or pull it back. Don't place him tummy up, because he would have to turn his head to the side to nurse. Just try to swallow with *your* head turned! Instead, turn his whole body to face you, his belly against your belly.

Never try to put a crying baby or a baby with a closed mouth to the breast. Wait until he is calm and has his mouth wide open. If you put him to the breast before his mouth is open, he will not latch on well. This will cause sore nipples. A newborn baby has a strong rooting reflex that makes him turn his head and open his mouth when touched lightly on the cheek. Touch him lightly with a finger on the side nearest the nipple to help him find it (see opposite page). Sometimes, if you express a drop of colostrum, you can trigger his interest because he will notice its sweet smell.

When your baby's mouth is open, bring him to the breast. Don't try to bring the breast to him. It would cause you to stoop and could create back problems. And he won't latch on as well. Don't try to push his head toward you or have someone hold the back of his head. This will make him push his head back into the touch instead of towards the breast. Just bring your arm closer to bring him to the breast. Aim him so that his lower lip is far down on the areola, the colored part around the nipple. Or think of it as aiming him so the nipple points at the roof of his mouth. He will then latch on and begin to suck.

You may feel surprised at the feeling of his first sucking, which may be quite strong. It is his instinct to suck. But he learns quickly, too. He learns that colostrum, and then milk, comes from the sucking. In a very short time, he learns that when he is hungry and put in the position to nurse, he can stop crying and find the nipple.

How often?

Nurse your baby whenever she seems to want to nurse. Some new babies want to be at the breast for much of the time in the first few days. All this sucking may help your milk come in more quickly. Other babies are rather sleepy. Those who still have some drugs in their system from the birth may not have a strong urge to suck. Take your cue from your baby. Put her to the breast whenever she wakes during the first few days.

After the milk comes in, the supply will settle down to match your baby's needs. Then she may have longer breaks between feedings. Breast milk is easy to digest. Her stomach will often be empty two to three hours after a feeding. Or she may want to nurse just 15 minutes after the last feeding. She may just be thirsty and want only the foremilk this time. Or it may be that she is in a growth spurt and her appetite has increased. Put her to the breast again to satisfy her for now. A day or two of frequent feedings will increase your milk supply. Then her needs will be met with fewer, larger feedings again.

At first, and later on, a breast-fed baby will let you know how often she needs to nurse. You can trust her messages. If in doubt, offer the breast. If it's not really what she needs, she may not nurse. Or, she may nurse for just a short time.

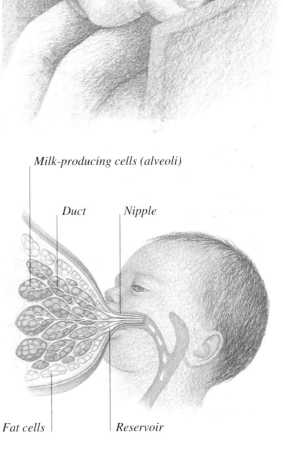

Above: To help your baby latch on, stroke his cheek gently on the side nearest the nipple.
Right: Get yourself comfortable to breast-feed, with your back straight. It helps to put a pillow under a very young baby.

Above: To release the nipple in the middle of a feeding, insert the tip of your finger gently into the corner of your baby's mouth.
Right: In response to your baby sucking, milk travels from the milk-producing cells (alveoli) down the ducts to the nipple.

Milk-producing cells (alveoli)

Duct   Nipple

Fat cells   Reservoir

How long?

There is no need to limit the amount of time at the breast. Your baby is not really sucking on the nipple, but just holding it back in her mouth. Your nipple will not become sore from the time she spends on the breast. Let her stay as long as she likes. She will stop when she is finished.

It is true that you may have some soreness in the first few days, before the nipple skin toughens up. It often feels worst when the baby first latches on and then a little better after the milk lets down. For many women, this is thankfully just a short-lived process that must be gone through. You can't prevent it by limiting the time at each breast to just a few minutes. In fact, if your baby sucks as long as she likes, you may get over the soreness more quickly. Sore nipples can also mean that the baby is not latching on correctly. If soreness persists, see a lactation consultant. When the baby is in the right position, nursing shouldn't hurt.

Don't remove your baby from the breast before she is ready to stop nursing. The letdown of the richer hindmilk may not happen until a few minutes into a feeding. If you change breasts or stop nursing before the letdown occurs, your baby will not receive the rich hindmilk. Too much sweet foremilk can give a baby gas pains. So let her have as much as she likes from one side. Then you can offer her the other breast, in case she wants to finish with a drink of sweet foremilk.

TIPS FOR BREAST-FEEDING

- *If milk drips from the other breast while your baby nurses, press firmly against the nipple with your hand. This may stop the flow.*
- *Tops you can pull up make nursing in public discreet.*
- *Most women prefer nursing bras that fully open from the front rather than just dropping a flap. They are less likely to cause a blocked duct by putting pressure on the breast.*
- *Drugs may be passed on through your milk to your baby. Be sure your doctor knows you are breast-feeding. Ask the pharmacist about the safety of any over-the-counter medicines before you take them.*
- *Your baby does not need extra water to drink, even in hot weather. Just nurse more often.*
- *Some babies react to certain foods in your diet with a crying, colicky spell.*
- *You can check for reactions by not eating a food you suspect. Then try it again after a couple of weeks.*
- *Don't switch to bottle-feeding because you are tired. You might find yourself just as tired, but with even more work to do preparing bottles. Rest is the key for all new mothers, breast-feeding or not.*

If she still seems hungry after the second breast, you can change her back to the first again. There will have been a further letdown of milk and more will now be ready.

You don't need to nurse from both breasts at each feeding. If your baby seems full with just one breast, start with the more full breast next time. This way both breasts are emptied fairly often and will keep producing milk.

If you do need to interrupt a feeding for any reason, don't just pull your baby off the breast. This can make your nipples sore. Break the suction first by pulling down gently on her chin. Or slip a finger inside the corner of her mouth (see page 55).

Enough milk

As long as you nurse your baby whenever he is hungry, you should have no problem making enough milk. Size and shape of breasts make no difference. Breast size depends upon layers of fat around the milk-producing cells. Even the smallest breasts can make just as much milk.

Sometimes women worry that their milk is of poor quality. It will look thinner and bluish-white after the first few days. That is how breast milk looks after it slowly changes from creamy-looking colostrum. And it is exactly right. Another cause for worry can be when the breasts do not feel full. When your milk first comes in, the breasts are very full and look huge. But after a few weeks, your breasts settle down to make just enough milk for your baby's needs. Your breasts may remain soft and never feel full. But they will be making much more milk than in the early days.

If your baby seems fussy or still hungry after nursing, don't be tempted to fill him up with a bottle. Formula milk digests more slowly than breast milk. This means he won't want to nurse at your breast as long as usual. Your breasts won't get the stimulation they need to make more milk. Also, the thought that a bottle at night will give you a chance to rest and make more milk is false. Breast-feeding at night is especially important. Nursing at night can boost your milk supply even more than nursing during the day. Remember that breast-feeding is a system of supply and demand. If your baby takes formula from a bottle, your breasts will make that much less milk.

Instead, keep switching your baby back to the other breast when he has finished with one. He will receive more milk, and your breasts will start making more. You may find that he needs to nurse again fairly soon. But if you nurse him often for a day or two, your supply will soon catch up.

Rest and good food

You have to get enough rest to produce milk well. Don't rush around too much. Try to have a nap or at least put your feet up each afternoon. Breast-feeding hormones will help you relax. They help you sleep better at night, too.

BREAST-FEEDING – POSSIBLE PROBLEMS

You may have few or none of the problems listed below. But some troubles are common in the early weeks. Many can be solved with help from a lactation consultant or a La Leche League leader. Most of the time breast-feeding settles down to become a simple pleasure.

PROBLEM	CAUSE	WHAT TO DO
Engorgement	Breasts overfull as milk comes in, or from missing feedings.	Nurse baby often to keep up your milk supply. A warm shower before nursing can soften breasts and helps baby latch on. Express a little milk to help baby grasp nipple. Cold compresses after nursing relieve swelling.
Afterpains	Hormones released in nursing cause uterus to contract. These may be painful in the early days. Pains are often worse with second or later babies.	Try to relax and breathe deeply. These contractions will get your uterus back to normal quickly. Beware of painkillers. They will be passed on in your milk.
Sore nipples	Pain at start of a feeding caused by suction.	This is a normal feeling. It will soon lessen or stop.
	Pain throughout a feeding. Baby not latched on properly.	Wrong nursing position. Ask a lactation consultant or a Le Leche League leader to see if baby is latched on correctly.
	Breasts sensitive to soap, creams or sprays.	Don't use products on nipples. Plain water is enough. Dry cornstarch can be soothing.
	Nipples wet.	Remove soggy breast pads. If plastic-lined, they may keep nipples too wet. Expose nipples to air as much as possible.
Cracked nipple	May develop from a sore nipple. Often caused by baby not latching on properly.	If very painful to nurse, rest breast for one or two feedings. Express milk and nurse from other side. Nipple shields may help.

PROBLEM	CAUSE	WHAT TO DO
Inverted or flat nipple	Your natural shape may mean the nipple is hard for the baby to grasp.	Contact a lactation consultant or La Leche League leader during pregnancy or soon after birth. If the baby's position is right at the breast, his sucking will pull out flat or inverted nipples.
Tender lump in breast; feels red and hot	Blocked duct.	Continue to nurse often. Put a damp, hot washcloth on the sore place often and before nursing. Massage sore breast in a hot bath or shower before nursing. Change baby's position during feedings to be sure the whole breast is emptied. Be sure bra or clothing doesn't press on breast. Don't wear a bra when you sleep.
Same as for blocked duct, but also flu-like signs	Mastitis, an infection in the breast. May be from germs entering nipple crack, or milk left in overfull breasts.	See your doctor. You may need antibiotics. Keep nursing unless your doctor advises not to. Express milk if not nursing. Follow other advice as for blocked duct.
Baby not gaining weight	Baby may be ill.	Have doctor check baby.
	No letdown of milk.	Relax when nursing. Put a warm washcloth on breasts before nursing. Don't limit the time at each breast. Make sure baby is latched on. Meet with a lactation consultant or La Leche League leader.
	Use of pacifier or bottles decreases sucking at breast.	Cut them out. Increase nursing at the breast instead.
	Not feeding baby enough.	Boost milk supply with frequent feedings, rest and good diet. Bottle-feed only after breast-feeding and only if there is no sign of improvement.

BOTTLE-FEEDING

There are many reasons why you may decide to bottle-feed your baby. You can expect your baby to thrive on the formula milk available. You may decide from the start that you want to use a bottle. Or you may start out breast-feeding and then switch. It helps your baby to receive the first food from the breast. Colostrum provides immune protection and guards against digestive problems. So you might want to start at the breast in any case. If all goes smoothly, you may want to stay with breast-feeding. If you do switch to bottles quite soon, your baby has still had a good start that formula milk can't provide.

Many mothers switch to bottles before they really want to. Problems with breast-feeding can make you feel frustrated or angry. Although a lot is said about the benefits of breast-feeding, you may not find much help with problems. If you are having problems and want to keep breast-feeding, contact a lactation consultant or a La Leche League leader (see Appendix). These women are experts. They are familiar with mothers' points of view and can give you help and advice.

There are times when it may be possible to solve most breast-feeding problems, but it may not be worth the effort and worry it can cause you. You need to feel happy, relaxed and confident about feeding your baby. Only you can know how the balance falls for you and your baby. Give yourself credit for making the best choice for both of you.

Why bottle-feed?

Sharing feeding: With bottle-feeding, the baby's father can give feedings. Other family members can, too. The mother is less tied down. She can be more flexible about her own time if she knows her baby can be fed by someone else in her absence.

Going back to work: If you plan to go back to work, you will need someone else to feed your baby. If you rent a good electric breast pump, it's easy to pump and store your milk in the freezer (see Appendix). This way your baby can keep receiving the benefits of breast milk. Contact a lactation consultant or La Leche League (see Appendix) to learn how to store breast milk. If you start your baby on the breast, try a bottle containing your expressed breast milk now and then. She should get used to taking milk from a bottle before you go back to work.

Social or family pressures: In some families, bottle-feeding is the norm. You might feel self-conscious about breast-feeding. Or perhaps your husband doesn't want you to breast-feed. Some women worry about feeding their baby in public when they are out. With these sorts of pressures, you might feel better about feeding with a bottle.

"In the early weeks when Carol was breast-feeding, I sometimes felt jealous that there was nothing I could do. And I couldn't help at night when she was tired. But after eight or ten weeks we sometimes gave him a bottle. It was nice for me to be able to feed him." PETER

A feeding is a time of closeness and sharing. Your baby might like you to talk or hum to her. Some hungry babies feed steadily. Others prefer to break off for a smile and a little "chat" before going back to their milk.

Physical reasons: The mother may have a physical condition, such as an illness. She may need to take medications that would appear in breast milk. Other problems may make nursing difficult and don't improve with time. Certain problems in the baby, such as cleft palate, may preclude breast-feeding or make it difficult.

Emotional reasons: Some women simply don't like the thought of breast-feeding. Or they may not feel good about having a baby so closely dependent, attached and intimate in nursing. There is no point in breast-feeding and feeling unhappy if you can feel warm and loving by giving a bottle.

Choosing a formula

Formula milk is often made from cow's milk. Some are based on soy protein. There are many differences between cow's milk and human milk. Baby formula is as close as possible to breast milk in the amount of protein, fats, carbohydrates, vitamins and minerals. Because a calf grows much more quickly than a baby, cow's milk contains three times more protein. It is diluted to make infant formula. The protein is also a different type, called *casein*. Casein is bulky and hard for a baby to digest. Cow's-milk proteins are processed to make them easier to digest. But the milk still takes longer for a baby to digest. That's why a bottle-fed baby tends to go about four hours between feedings instead of two or three for a breast-fed baby.

Formula milk also contains added sugars to match the amount of milk sugar in breast milk. Minerals are removed so there will not be a strain on the baby's kidneys. Skim milk and certain vegetable oils are also added. Formula makers try to come close to the types of fat found in breast milk.

There are many different brands and types of formula. Any type of infant formula will likely be suitable. It is best to choose one type and stick with it, rather than change back and forth. If you think there may be a problem with the formula, discuss it with your doctor.

Some babies are allergic to the cow's milk protein in formula. You may need to use a soy-based formula. But your baby may also be allergic to soy proteins. So don't make a change without consulting your doctor.

Equipment

You will need six to eight bottles. They should be unbreakable, with wide necks for easy cleaning. And you'll need about a dozen rubber nipples. You might want to look for nipples that are shaped to copy the sucking action of breast-feeding. Sometimes called "orthodontic" nipples, these may be better for the baby's growing jaw. Such nipples can make it easier if you want to combine breast- and bottle-feeding. You will also need sterilizing equipment. This will include a sterilizing bath and tablets, a bottle brush, measuring pitcher, long-handled spoon and a knife.

Sterilizing

You must sterilize everything you use to fix formula and feed your baby for at least the first four months. Milk is a perfect place for germs to grow. Your baby could easily become ill if all the germs are not destroyed.

First wash bottles carefully in warm, soapy water. Clean the inside with a brush to remove all traces of formula. Rub the inside of the nipples with salt and rinse them well. When the items are clean, they can be sterilized.

The most common way to sterilize equipment is in a large unit filled with water. Dissolve a sterilizing tablet in the water or add sterilizing fluid. Follow the directions as to how long items must be left in the solution. Everything must be fully submerged. Make sure there are no air bubbles in bottles or nipples. Once they have been in the solution for the correct time, you may want to rinse with boiled water. This will remove the chlorine and its strong smell. Or, you can sterilize bottles and the measuring cup in a normal dish-washer cycle. Use tablets to sterilize nipples. Some sterilizing units work in a microwave. There are also steam sterilizers (electric units for sealed sterilizing of equipment). Follow the instructions for use.

Making up bottles

It will save time if you make up all the bottles you may need for a day at one time. First wash your hands well. Boil the water you will use. Then allow it to

- *If your breasts become engorged when your milk comes in, a bra with good support will help. Discomfort may last a day or two. Your doctor can prescribe a drug to stop your milk production.*
- *Cooled boiled water can be offered between feedings if your baby is thirsty. Do not use sweetened herbal or fruity drinks. These can decay baby teeth.*
- *Don't leave your baby with a propped-up bottle. This can cause choking. Besides, your baby needs you.*
- *Once milk is warmed, feed your baby right away. There should be no time for germs to build up.*
- *Never use an insulated bottle to keep milk warm. This is a perfect breeding ground for germs. If you are going out, you could keep warm boiled water in an insulated bottle. Then add it to the milk powder in a sterilized bottle when needed.*
- *Changing sides halfway through a feeding gives your arms a rest. It also gives your baby a different view of the world.*

cool to lukewarm before pouring it into the sterile pitcher. Check the formula can to figure out how much you need to mix for your baby's age and weight. It's good to put a little more than you expect your baby will want into each bottle. If she is very hungry, you won't have to start on another bottle. Any leftovers must be thrown away.

Measure the required number of scoops of powder. Level each with the sterile knife before you add the powder to the water in the jug. You must use level scoops. Never add extra scoops! Milk that is too strong will strain or damage your baby's kidneys and will make her thirsty. Stir well with the sterilized spoon until the powder is dissolved. Then pour the milk into the sterile bottles. Place the nipples upside down into the bottles, and secure with the lids. Then put the filled bottles into the refrigerator right away. Keep them there until ready for use. If you use liquid formula, wash the lid well before opening. Use a sterile can opener and equipment as above.

When to feed your baby

Feed your baby whenever she is hungry. If you have decided to bottle-feed right from the start, your baby's first feeding may be sugared water. She may not be very hungry in the first day or two. But feed her when she cries. Soon she may settle into roughly 4-hour intervals between feedings. There will be times, though, when she sleeps longer. She may also want more feedings in a day. Take your cue from her.

Bottle-feeding your baby

Settle yourself with your baby. Be sure you are sitting with your back straight to prevent strain and fatigue. This is a time for you both to enjoy. Give her all your attention. Stroke her cheek nearest you so she will turn to find the nipple and be ready to suck. Then gently slide the nipple into her mouth. Hold the bottle tilted so the nipple is filled with milk. The milk should flow well so she won't swallow air.

Feeding is a social time, so look at your baby. Talk to her or hum or sing to her. She might want to take a break from her feeding and then come back to it. Let her set the pace.

Halfway through the feeding, it's good to burp your baby. This helps her bring up any air she might have swallowed. If she pauses, she may need to burp. Then she can drink her fill. Put a cloth over your shoulder. Hold her upright against your shoulder. Gently stroke or pat her back. Lay her across your lap, tummy down, and pat her back. Or support her upright on your lap in a sitting position while you rub or pat her back (see page 25).

Let your baby decide when she has had enough. Don't coax her to finish a bottle. You could get her too full so she throws up the milk. Or she could become overweight. Just throw out any milk left in the bottle at the end of a feeding. If she finishes a bottle and wants more, you can go on to another bottle. But throw out any she leaves in the bottle. Put more in the bottles if she tends to finish feedings and is fussy or hungry again after only a couple of hours.

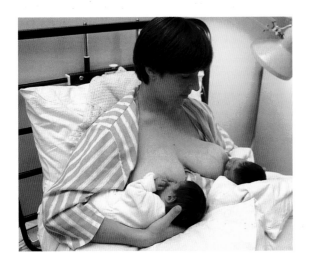

Twins can be fully breast-fed. Either feed both at once or one after the other. The position shown here works well. Or one baby can lie across the mother's front, with the other at her side. The extra sucking signals the breasts to make enough milk for two babies.

QUESTIONS AND ANSWERS

Q: I will be going back to work when my baby is a few weeks old. I don't want to give up breast-feeding totally. Is it possible to do both?

A: Yes, you can combine breast- and bottle-feeding. It's not a good idea to combine the two right at the start. First you have to get breast-feeding established. But after you begin work, your milk supply will soon adjust to the amount your baby takes if you nurse your baby just in the morning and evening. Begin with a bottle before you go back to work, in time to get your baby used to taking milk from a rubber nipple.

Q: Is it possible to breast-feed twins?

A: Twins can be fully breast-fed. Mothers of twins often feed both babies at one time. Sit up with a baby at each breast or lay them alongside with their feet toward your back (see opposite page). Another approach is to feed one baby when it wakes. Then wake and feed the other so it is still really one feeding session. A breast-feeding mother of twins needs an excellent diet and lots of help so she can get enough rest.

Q: My baby throws up lots of milk. Is he getting enough nourishment?

A: See your doctor to rule out possible problems. But the answer will likely be that it is nothing to worry about. The valve at the entrance to the stomach is very loose in young babies. Milk can come out nearly as easily as it goes in. Some babies do throw up milk very freely. It is messy but does no harm. Feed your baby when he is hungry. If he is contented, alert and sociable, it is likely he is getting enough milk. If you are bottle-feeding, be careful not to coax him into taking too much. Keep plenty of cloths handy for mopping up. It might help to prop up your baby at an angle for a while after feedings. He will outgrow this behavior in time.

Q: Do I need to warm my baby's bottle?

A: Your baby's bottle does not have to be warm. But most babies seem to prefer warm milk. You can use a bottle warmer. Or just stand the bottle in a bowl of hot water or hold it under the hot tap. Don't use a microwave. The milk can get too hot while the bottle still feels cool. There can also be uneven hot spots in the milk. If you do use a microwave, shake the bottle well to mix the milk and disperse heat. However you heat a bottle, always check the temperature of the milk before giving it to your baby. Let a few drops fall on the inside of your wrist. The milk should be body temperature and not hot.

Q: How should I check the flow of milk from the nipple?

A: With the bottle tipped, there should be a steady drip from the nipple. If it comes in a stream, the hole is too big. Your baby will sputter and choke. If it doesn't drip at all, or only slowly, the hole is too small. Your baby will work too hard to be fed. You can enlarge the hole with a needle heated to red-hot, which will melt the rubber.

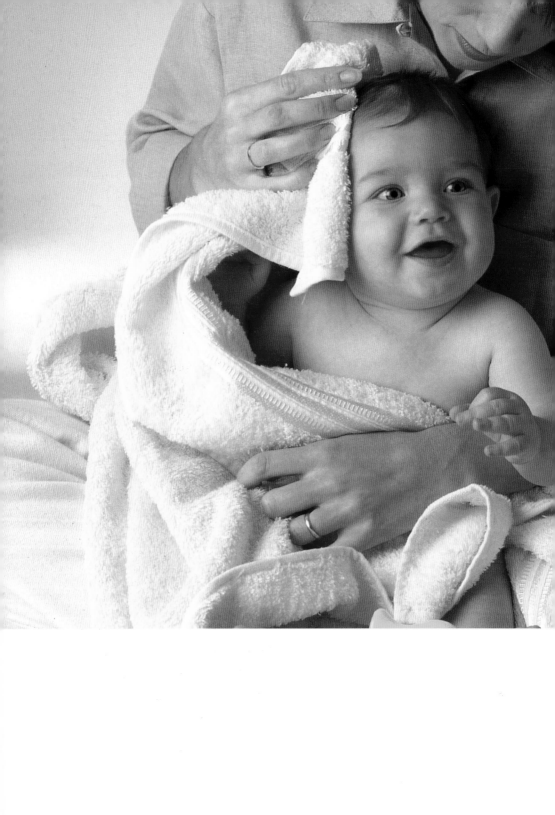

5

Clean and Comfortable

When I got baby clothes before Robert was born, my husband joked that I just wanted to play dolls. It is fun to dress him up to show him off. But mostly it's a matter of lots of changes because he's dribbled milk or leaked around his diaper.

CHANGING NEEDS

Newborns spend most of the day sleeping in a crib or cradled in your arms. In just a few months, your baby will turn into a crawling explorer. He will go all over and put whatever he finds straight into his mouth. The task of keeping him clean and comfortable keeps changing.

DIAPERS

Your baby will be taking true milk feedings after the first few days. After that you can expect from six to 12 wet diapers per day. As your baby grows, he will stay dry longer because the bladder can hold more before it empties.

When do diapers need changing?

A baby's urine is pale, not strong, and sterile. Most of the time it does no harm to leave him wet for a while as long as the diaper is not soiled. Some babies don't like being wet. If your baby complains, then change him.

Dirty diapers need changing promptly. The stool is full of germs that act on urine to form ammonia. This irritates tender skin and causes diaper rash. Your baby's first bowel movement contains *meconium*, a dark, sticky, tar-like substance that has been in the bowel since before birth. Over the next few days, the stools will change to those of a milk-fed baby.

If your baby is breast-fed, his stools will be from almost liquid to soft and pasty. They will vary in color from a typical mustard yellow to greenish. Because breast milk is so well absorbed, your baby may have a bowel movement every few days. If the stool is soft when it appears, this is normal. It is also normal for a breast-fed baby to have a few bowel movements a day. This is often a reflex action triggered by a feeding. Diarrhea is pretty rare in breast-fed babies. Don't worry about frequent movements unless the stool is watery and there are other signs of illness.

A bottle-fed baby's stools will often be more formed and brownish in color. Formula milk stays longer in the gut, so these stools will have a stronger smell. There should be at least one bowel movement per day. A bottle-fed baby may become constipated. But judge this by the hardness of the stool, not by how often they happen. If you think your baby may be constipated, be sure you are not adding too much milk powder to bottles. Offer cooled boiled water for drinks between feedings. If the problem persists, see your doctor.

When a young baby wakes crying with hunger, feed him before you change him. If you change him first, he may become frantic. Then it can be hard to settle him down for a feeding. He will often need changing afterwards anyway. So just wait to change him after the feeding. During the night, some parents like to change a

" It helps if you own a laundry! We've been running the washing machine at least twice a day. " ANDREW

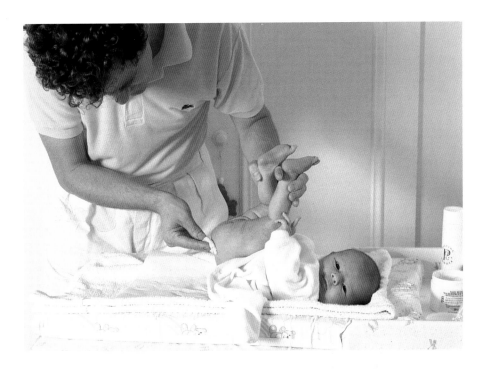

baby in the middle of a feeding. This lets him doze off in the second half without being roused by changing afterwards. An older baby will learn that once you are there his feeding won't be far behind. In time, you can change him first and he can be fed in comfort.

What kind of diapers?

Choosing diapers means weighing the pros and cons. Ask other mothers. If you're not sure, start with disposables. They are easy to use with a new baby. Make up your mind when you are a bit more settled.

Disposables are also easy when traveling. You might like to use them then, no matter what you use at home.

Plain water on a cotton ball is enough to clean your baby if her diaper is only wet. Lotion may make the job easier when she is soiled. Diaper ointment helps if your baby's skin is very sensitive. But don't use powders. Powder dust can be harmful to the baby if inhaled.

Cotton cloth diapers: The old-fashioned cotton cloth diaper has some benefits. Price is one. Though they cost more at first, you don't have to keep buying diapers. They can also be handed down to a later baby. When folded in one of a few styles, they can fit your baby well. Some parents like the fact that they are a natural fabric. They are also kinder to the environment than disposables. They're not made from trees. And they don't cause waste-disposal problems.

But they are more work to use than disposables. And they are bulky for a baby to wear. Quite a bit of work is involved in sterilizing, washing and folding. (And washing and cleaning chemicals are not good for the environment.) Shaped cloth diapers are also available. These have a thick central absorbent layer and thinner cloth on the sides. These may fit your baby better but they take longer to dry.

If you decide on cloth diapers, you will need at least 24 to allow for washing and drying time. You will also need waterproof pants and safety pins with locking heads. Paper diaper liners are softer for your baby and make changing simpler. One-way liners draw moisture away from your baby's skin to keep him drier. (See opposite page for folding a cloth diaper.)

Reusables: You may try washable, reusable diapers. They are cheaper and better for the environment than disposables. They can last for more than one baby. Compared to regular cloth diapers, they are easier to use. They look and fit better. They are machine-washable and can be tumble-dried. But they take around 24 hours to line dry.

A few styles are available. Some have waterproof pants with cloth lining and absorbent padding. Most have elastic legs and Velcro® waist fasteners. Two-piece versions include shaped cloth diapers with separate outer waterproof pants. Some waterproof pants or wraps have pockets to hold absorbent pads.

Disposables: Disposable diapers are most convenient. You just have to shop frequently for bulky packages. There are sizes to fit every baby, from low birthweight to a toddler's overnight size. Most offer a good fit, with reusable waist tapes and elastic legs. A one-way lining keeps baby's skin dry. And they absorb well. Different styles are made for girls and boys.

Disposables are easy to use and require no washing. Care must be taken in disposing of soiled diapers. Put the diaper in a plastic bag and seal it before putting it out in the trash.

Washing diapers

If you use washable diapers, good hygiene will help protect your baby from diaper rash. If soiled, hold the diaper in the toilet as you flush to rinse it through. Then drop it to soak, with other wet diapers, in a bucket. Half-fill the bucket every day with a germ-killing solution. Keep a lid on the bucket until you are ready for the daily diaper wash. Don't wash diapers with other clothes. Don't use a biological detergent. They can irritate your baby's skin. Dry and air diapers well before use.

Diaper service

A diaper service is a simpler way to use cloth diapers. A service can cost about the same as disposables. The service does the laundry. You purchase the diapers with the service, so you will always be using the same diapers. Just

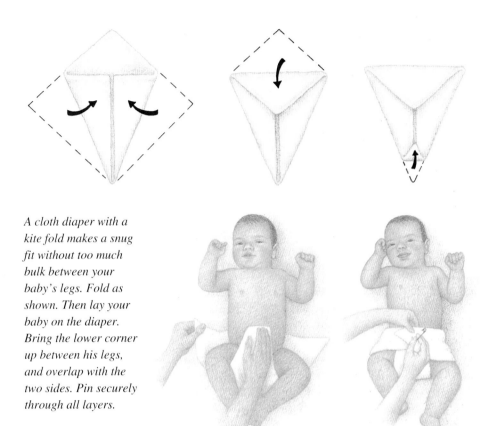

A cloth diaper with a kite fold makes a snug fit without too much bulk between your baby's legs. Fold as shown. Then lay your baby on the diaper. Bring the lower corner up between his legs, and overlap with the two sides. Pin securely through all layers.

TIPS FOR DIAPER CHANGING

◆ *Fifteen minutes without a diaper promotes healthy skin. If you have a baby boy, keep a cloth handy to toss over him if he pees.*

◆ *Close diaper pins as soon as you take them off. It's safer in case the baby grabs one.*

◆ *When pinning a diaper, slide your fingers between the pin and your baby. This way you can't prick him by mistake.*

◆ *Clean ointment from your fingers before closing the tapes on a disposable, or they won't stick.*

◆ *Don't leave your baby up on a changing surface even for a second. She may give no warning before she learns to roll over.*

◆ *If the diaper doesn't leak and leave your baby wet and cold, and he doesn't have a rash, you don't need to change him at night if he is just wet.*

follow the instructions for dealing with wet and soiled diapers. The service will pick up and deliver once or twice each week.

Changing time

You need a flat, firm surface for changing your baby. A padded changing mat you can sponge off is handy. But a towel works just as well. Put it on the floor, on a bed or sofa, or on top of a chest of drawers. Have all the things you'll need. You won't want to leave your baby for an instant once you've started. You might like to have one permanent changing station. A basket or bag with all your things in it makes changing in other rooms easy.

You will need a clean diaper and the things you need for the type of diaper you use. You will also need clean cotton balls, a bowl of warm water, baby lotion or vegetable oil and maybe some diaper ointment. If the diaper has leaked, you will need a change of clothes. For an older baby, a toy or other object can help distract your baby from trying to escape the whole process.

Lay your baby on her back, and unfasten lower clothing. Remove socks or booties because she may kick into the dirty diaper. With one hand, hold her ankles with one finger between to keep them from rubbing together. Lift her legs and slide the clothing under her back well up out of the way.

Unfasten the dirty diaper. If it is soiled, use the unsoiled front part of the diaper to wipe away as much of the feces as you can. Then fold over the diaper and put it aside.

If your baby is just wet, plain water is all you need for wiping the diaper area. For a young baby, cotton balls are softest on delicate skin. After a few weeks, you can use plain toilet paper. If soiled, water may be enough. But it can be easier to clean off feces with a little baby lotion. A vegetable oil such as almond or olive oil works well, too.

To clean a baby girl, always wipe from front to back to keep germs away from the vagina. Never open the inner lips of the vulva to clean inside. The vagina stays clean by itself. Just clean the exposed genitals. You may need to gently spread the vulva to wipe it clean.

For a baby boy, wipe clean around the penis and then clean the genitals. Again, clean only the exposed parts. Don't pull back the foreskin. It may be at least three or four years before the foreskin is loose enough to pull back for cleaning underneath. If you try to do it too soon, you may cause small tears. Tears can result in adhesions. Circumcision, the surgical removal of the fore-skin, is sometimes performed on baby boys as a religious practice. It is rarely required for medical reasons. And it is never required on babies.

When the genital area is clean, lift your baby's legs and clean the bottom. Then pat the whole area dry. Pay special attention to the leg creases. They can become sore if left damp. You don't always need a diaper ointment. But if your baby has very sensitive skin or has diaper rash, you might try some. Don't use baby powder. Your baby could inhale some into his lungs. And powder tends to cake in skin creases, causing soreness.

Now you can put on a clean diaper and dress your baby again. Dispose of the used diaper. Then wash your hands well.

"Julia had a terrible case of thrush. The only way to clear it up was to use cloth diapers for a week. I also left her bare for the air to circulate. When the week was up, I thought 'Thank God!' Disposables are so much easier. I think they're awfully expensive, though. We'd like to live an environmentally friendly life. But we excuse ourselves by saying, 'Oh, well, we'll plant a couple of trees.'" RACHEL

A fun time?

Your baby's reaction to being changed will vary as she grows. Diaper changes provide a chance for you to spend time with her. Some new babies seem to hate being undressed. They are used to the close contact of the womb. Talk to your baby as you change her. If she is fussy and seems unhappy at the process, just work as gently and quickly as you can.

Later on she may enjoy a chat with you as you change her. She may also learn to like the feeling of freedom in being without her diaper. If she is happy being undressed, let her kick in the air for a while. It's good exercise for her. And it's good for her bottom to be exposed to air.

Once your baby learns to roll over and crawl or scoot, you'll have to keep her still long enough to be changed. You could hang a colorful mobile above your changing place. It also helps to talk to her. By nine or ten months, she might even like to "help." She can hold a lotion bottle or some tissue until you ask her for it.

Diaper rash

There is no sure way to prevent diaper rash (see page 74). Some babies have more sensitive skin than others. But any baby may get a rash. Prevent rashes with frequent changes and exposure to fresh air. Then it's harder for germs to work on urine to form stinging ammonia. If you use cloth diapers, one-way liners or a brief change to disposables might help clear up a rash. Or you could try rinsing diapers in a mild vinegar solution (1 cup to 1 gallon of water). The slight acidity slows down the growth of germs and neutralizes ammonia.

WASHING AND BATHING

Sometimes nothing else can be as refreshing and soothing as a bath. Bathing your baby can be a pleasure for you both. And once your baby learns to splash and pour, it can be great fun.

TYPES OF DIAPER RASH

Ammonia dermatitis: *A red rash in the diaper area, starting by the genitals. You may notice the strong smell of ammonia on the diaper.*
Caused by: *Ammonia formed from germs acting on urine.*
What to do: *More frequent diaper changes. Wash the area well. Expose bottom to air. Do not use soap, which can dry the skin. Use one-way liners or disposables to keep urine off the skin. Use a soothing diaper ointment.*

Thrush: *A painful red rash that starts around the anus and spreads to the buttocks. It tends to be worse in creases. Thrush can also appear in the mouth as white spots. It may cause pain and problems with feedings.*
Caused by: Candida albicans *fungal infection.*
What to do: *See your doctor. You will likely need an antifungal cream and perhaps medicine to take by mouth. Dry carefully and expose the skin to air.*

Sore in creases: *Red or broken skin in leg creases.*
Caused by: *Damp in creases after changing or bath.*
What to do: *Pat dry well. Don't rub delicate skin. Expose to air. Don't use powder. Diaper ointment may help.*

Persistent rash: *Rash that doesn't clear with normal measures.*
Caused by: *Possibly lanolin or other substance in soaps, lotions or baby wipes. May be a reaction of sensitive skin. Or it could be the natural balance of the skin is upset.*
What to do: *Don't use any products except water and a natural vegetable oil.*

For your young baby

A new baby doesn't get too dirty, except for the face and neck from dribbled milk, and the diaper area. So a daily full bath is not really needed. Clean face and bottom once or twice a day. A full wash every few days is enough. Some babies love being in a bath right from the start. Others may not enjoy a bath for weeks. If your baby cries and seems scared in the bath, don't use a bath at all. Just give a sponge bath on your lap. Your baby may feel better if she has a bath with you. If you are breast-feeding, you might get in the tub with her. Let her nurse while you bathe her.

For your older baby

Older babies need baths more often. Once on solid food, you may find bits of food from hair to feet. When she is mobile, she will get grubby from active life at ground level. Bathtime can be whenever you like. Many parents like to bathe their baby in the evening, before the last feeding.

Fathers can have a great time bathing the baby. This can give the mother a break if she has been caring for the baby all day. An evening bath also helps relax your baby and signals bedtime.

Before she can even sit up, your baby may learn that by arching her back and kicking she is able to make huge splashes. Once this happens, bathtime becomes lots more fun. She will enjoy splashing and playing with bath toys. Things that float or sink make great toys. Fill plastic bottles with water to squirt for her. And help her learn to pour.

Even shallow water is always a source of danger. So never leave your baby alone in the bath, even for a second. She could easily slip under or try to stand and fall. Keep a hand on her all the time until she is really good at sitting. If she topples and goes under, it can give her a bad scare. A bath mat can reduce the risk of your baby slipping.

Support your baby's head with your forearm while your hand keeps a firm grip on his shoulder and arm. This leaves your other hand free for washing your baby. Meanwhile, he enjoys lying, kicking or splashing in the warm water.

Face and bottom

For a quick cleaning of face, hands and bottom, you need warm water, cotton balls, a towel and diaper-changing things. Use a separate cotton ball for each eye. Wipe from the middle outwards. Wipe around each ear and the outside ear. But do not clean inside

the ears or put anything in them. Wipe the rest of the face. Clean the creases under the chin to remove any milk, which will irritate the skin. Dry well by patting gently. Wipe and dry the hands. Then remove your baby's diaper and clean as for any diaper change.

Sponge bath

For a sponge bath, you can wash your baby on a changing mat or on a towel in your lap. You will need a bowl of water, cotton balls, a washcloth, soap, shampoo, a towel and diaper-changing things. Clean your baby's face as above. Then remove clothes from the top of her body while the bottom stays dressed. Gently soap the front of her body. Then rinse with the washcloth and pat dry. Sit her up and lean her on your arm to repeat on her back. If you want to shampoo her hair, wet it with the cloth. Lather, then rinse well with the wet cloth. Then put on your baby's T-shirt. Remove the lower clothing and clean the diaper area. Then wash legs and feet and dress her.

Giving a bath

To give your baby a bath, first gather the things you will need. You won't be able to leave her once you have begun. You can use a plastic baby bathtub, which can be carried into any room. But be careful of your back. Bend your knees and not your back as you lift it and put it down. Or you can use a bathroom or kitchen sink, which may offer convenient counter space.

Move faucets out of the way or wrap them with a washcloth. You will need the same things as for a sponge bath. Fill the bath with just a few inches of water. The water should be warm, but not as warm as you would like for a

The bath becomes an exciting playground once your baby can sit up. Getting clean isn't nearly as fun as watching bubbles, catching a floating toy or making huge splashes. What could be better than pouring water from a bunch of cups and bottles?

- *Make sure you have everything you will need within easy reach before you begin.*
- *Use a nonslip mat, a washcloth or small towel in the bottom of the bath to keep your baby from sliding.*
- *Have a jug of hot water ready to top up the baby bath if it has cooled off too much before you are ready for it.*
- *Keep dry diapers, towel and a change of clothes handy but out of splashing distance.*
- *If your baby doesn't like the feeling of water being poured over her head, rinse with a wet washcloth instead. Or scoop water onto her head with your hand.*
- *In the bathtub, don't pull the plug until after your baby is out of the bath. The noise of water draining might frighten her.*

bath for yourself. Always check with your elbow that it is about as warm as your body before you put your baby in the water.

First remove your baby's diaper and clean the diaper area. Then undress her. Wrap her in a towel and clean her face. A young baby gets cold quite quickly in a bath. So keep the time in the water short. Shampoo her hair before putting her in. Hold her with her legs under your arm. Your forearm will support her back while your hand holds her head. With her head over the bath, wet, shampoo and rinse her hair (see page 78). You can shampoo an older baby in the bath.

To lower your baby into the bath, reach under her shoulders with your left hand (if you are right-handed). Your forearm should support her while your hand firmly grasps her shoulder and arm on the far side. With the other hand, lift her bottom as you firmly hold one thigh. Then lower her slowly into the bath. Talk to her to comfort her as she feels the water. Your left hand maintains a grip at all times. The right hand will be free to wash your baby (see page 75). When she is clean and rinsed, lift her out on to a large dry towel. Wrap her quickly and pat dry. Be careful to dry the creases well.

Sharing a bath

You might like to wash even a very young baby in the bathtub with you. You may both enjoy the skin-to-skin contact. And she may feel more relaxed resting on your lap in the bath. Your partner can hand your baby to you once you are in the water. Your partner can also take her from you and wrap her in a

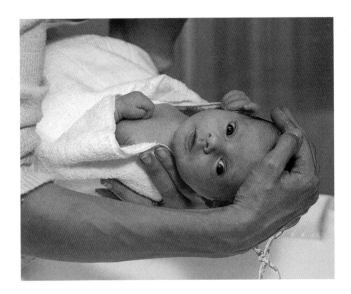

To keep your baby warm while you wash his hair, keep him wrapped snugly. Hold him with his head over the baby bath or sink to shampoo and rinse his hair. Then pat his head dry and follow with a full bath.

towel when you are done. But you can also manage on your own. First, clean your baby's face and diaper area. Wrap her in a towel and lay her on the floor beside the bath while you get in. Kneel in the bath to pick her up. Then settle into the bath together. If you are breast-feeding, nursing in the tub will comfort her. When you are ready to get out, kneel up and lower her on to the waiting towel. Wrap her up before you step out.

Care of:

Hair: Your baby may have little hair. It's still good to brush it daily with a soft brush to stimulate the scalp. You don't have to wash the hair with every bath. Once or twice a week with a gentle non-sting shampoo will keep it clean and may get rid of cradle cap. Don't be afraid to wash over the soft spots. They are covered with a tough membrane.

Nails: It's easy for a young baby to scratch herself with long fingernails. They need to be kept trimmed. You can use nail clippers. Special blunt-ended nail scissors may work best. Cut fingernails in a slightly rounded shape. Cut toenails straight across. After a bath, the nails are soft and easy to cut. Or you might prefer to cut them while your baby is asleep so she won't pull away.

Ears and nose: Both the ears and the nose are self-cleaning. There is no need to try to clean inside them. You could do damage by poking something into them. Just wipe away anything that appears on the outside.

DRESSING YOUR BABY

Dressing your baby is a practical matter. But it can also be fun. Choose clothes you like to see on your baby.

Temperature

The main purpose of clothing is to keep us warm. A baby should be dressed for comfort. Your baby is able to keep his body warm enough. Don't overdress him. This is as harmful as underdressing. But babies can't change their body temperatures quickly if there are rapid temperature changes around them. Your baby might need layers of clothing. Add or remove as you go from room to room or as the temperature changes. Your baby should be warm enough in the same number of layers that you are wearing. Check that he is warm but not too hot. Feel the back of his neck or his body. He should feel a bit warm, but not sweaty. Don't go by hands and feet. They might feel a little cooler even when he is warm enough.

First clothes

New babies often don't like getting dressed, so choose clothes that make dressing him easy. They should also be comfortable and simple to care for. Your baby will feel better in clothes made of natural fibers that "breathe." Cotton feels good next to the skin. A small bit of synthetic fiber with cotton may make the clothes easy to care for. They dry well with no need to iron.

Look for clothes that open at the front for easy changes. Snaps or Velcro fasteners make for easy fastening. Stretchy clothes are also easier to use and

DRESSING

- *Buy "three-months'-size" clothes rather than "newborn." They won't be outgrown as quickly.*
- *Don't buy too much. You may receive baby clothes as gifts. You can always add things later.*
- *Babies like strong bright colors, so don't choose all soft pastels.*
- *One-piece T-shirts with snaps between the legs are a great help. They keep T-shirts from riding up over your baby's tummy.*
- *A shawl is useful for wrapping your baby. But don't choose lacy patterns with holes. These can snag tiny fingers.*
- *Take a full change of clothes for your baby when you go out.*
- *Both parents should dress their baby. Let your partner learn to do it in his own way, even if you don't like the clothes he selects. Your baby doesn't mind how he looks, but loves having both parents involved.*

66 *Felicity wore blue for the first year because I'd gotten used baby clothes from my sister. People would say 'What's his name?' But I didn't want to dress her up. She spit up a lot and I just gave up. Dresses aren't very practical anyway.* 99 ANNE

feel better to your baby. Things that must go over the head should have a wide neck. Look for an envelope neck or snaps that open along the shoulder.

For a young baby, stretchsuits are a great wardrobe basic. They feel good and are easy to launder and use. And they can be worn with other thin layers such as T-shirts and sweaters. They can be worn day and night, although you may prefer nightgowns, which make night changes simpler. Don't use open-weave knitwear. Young babies tend to trap their fingers in the holes. Clothes with fringe or ribbons can be a problem because your baby may suck on them. Keep an eye on buttons to make sure they are sewn on firmly. Loose buttons can be a choking hazard.

A young baby grows quickly. Don't buy much in the first size. Your baby won't mind being dressed in clothes that are a bit too large. But watch out for fit. Pressure on tiny feet from pajamas with feet that are too short, or too-small socks, can damage the soft bones of the feet. Make sure there is plenty of room. To lengthen the life of pajamas with feet, cut off the feet and use socks with it instead.

Active clothes

Once your baby begins to crawl, you need tougher clothes. Look for those that protect the knees. Dresses for a girl can catch under her knees and stop her from crawling. Jeans and sweat suits are a better bet.

When a baby starts to walk, his clothes still need to be sturdy. They should also be loose enough to allow free movement. Layers that can be added or taken off still work well. Your baby will warm up when he is active.

Sun protection

In warm weather, it is nice for a baby to enjoy being outdoors. But watch out for the sun. Your baby's skin does not have much pigment to protect it from the sun. It can burn and be damaged very quickly. Use a high sun-protection-factor (spf) sunscreen and a hat with a brim. Light cotton clothing can protect your baby's delicate skin in hot weather.

Dressing your young baby

Dress your baby as he lies on his back or sits in your lap. Wrap him in a towel if he's just had a bath. Or keep him partly dressed while you put on one thing at a time.

He won't like clothes being pulled over his head. So be careful as you pull T-shirts or tops over his head. To remove a T-shirt, pull up the body. Then stretch open the armholes as you bend his elbow to guide his arms out first.

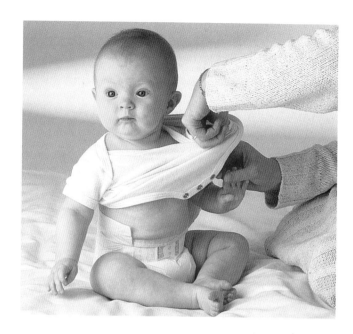

You will soon become expert at dressing your baby. Take a shirt and stretch the neck wide to slip it over your baby's head. Or reach into the sleeve to draw her hand through. Before long, she'll be helping you, too.

Then stretch the T-shirt neck hole open wide. Talk to him to comfort him as you slip it over his head. Be careful not to touch his face. Then slide it out from under his neck. When you put a T-shirt on your baby, roll up the trunk portion into a narrow strip and stretch the neck hole open. Put the T-shirt on over the back of your baby's head first. Then stretch it wide to clear his face as you pull it forward.

To put on sleeves, reach into the sleeve from the wrong end first. Grasp your baby's hand and slip on the sleeve. With a stretchsuit or sweater, roll up the sleeve to be as short as possible. Guide your baby's hand through it. Then straighten the sleeve along his arm.

To put on pajamas with feet, open it fully and lay your baby on it. Put on the arms first; then fasten the snaps for the front and legs.

Dressing your older baby

By the time your baby is a few months old, he may begin to help you get him dressed. He will stretch his arm to push it through a sleeve. This is the first step toward being able to dress himself. Encourage him to take part. Talk to him about what you are doing, step by step: "Let me have your hand. Push . . . good! Now the other one." It takes longer to involve him. But you will both enjoy it. And you will be teaching him to care for himself. So make him a partner when you get him dressed. Don't force clothes on him without letting him help or against his will.

He may prefer you to dress him as he sits or stands. Hold him on your lap or between your knees as you kneel. He can stand up as you pull up pants or trousers. By 18 months, he may be able to pull off some of his clothes by himself. And he may push his feet into shoes. You can sit him on a step and open his shoes in front of him. Then he can put his feet into them himself.

Be sure to protect your baby's delicate skin from the sun's harmful rays. Use cool clothing and sunscreen.

QUESTIONS AND ANSWERS

Q: My baby has cradle cap, even though I keep his hair clean. How can I clear it up and keep it from coming back?

A: Cradle cap is a common skin condition. Dry, scaly crusts form on the scalp. It is caused when glands in a newborn's scalp produce too much oil. It is harmless, but ugly. Shampoo has little effect. You may be tempted to remove any crusts that form. Never try to pick off the crusts. You could tear the skin beneath and cause infection. The crusts can be softened by rubbing a little olive oil into the scalp and leaving it for a few hours or overnight. Then you can gently remove the crusts with a fine-toothed comb. Follow with a thorough shampoo. It does tend to come back. If so, just do the same things again.

Q: When I put a soft wool sweater on my baby, her skin got red. Does this mean she is allergic to wool?

A: Some young babies are sensitive to wool. Wool may irritate their skin. But this is not an allergy. You may be able to use wool if it is not in direct contact with your baby's skin. Try putting on cotton underneath. Or just wait a few weeks and try again. She may outgrow the sensitive stage.

Q: Should I buy shoes for my baby now that she is pulling herself up to stand?

A: Feet grow best when they are not restrained in shoes. Even slight distortions in the soft bones early in life can cause problems later on. Socks or booties with plenty of room are all your baby needs until she begins to walk. Even then, she will need shoes only when walking outside. Indoors, soft fabric boots with grips on the soles are a good choice.

When you buy shoes, be sure your baby is fitted by a trained fitter who checks both length and width. The foot should not slip in the shoe or be under pressure. Choose shoes with nonslip soles that are flexible, not rigid. There are many good-looking baby-shoe styles. But foot health comes first.

Q: When will my baby be ready to start potty training?

A: He won't be a baby at all. By the time he is ready to start, he will be a toddler. You may learn when your baby is likely to fill his diaper. Put him on the potty at those times. But he won't be ready to learn for himself for some time. He has to mature enough to notice what is happening. He also has to be aware in advance and to signal to you that he needs the potty in time to get there. Most children are between 18 months and 2-1/2 years old before all these things come together.

6

Sleep

❝ People sometimes ask me, 'Is she a good baby?' I know what they really mean is, does she sleep a lot? Well, of course she's good. It goes without saying that all babies are good. But no, she doesn't sleep nearly as much as I wish she would. And I'm exhausted. ❞

WHAT PARENTS EXPECT

Few aspects of life with a baby have as much impact as the question of sleep. When does your baby sleep? How much does she sleep? And what happens when she doesn't sleep? Her sleep pattern becomes the center of your lives. You adjust your own sleep, and your day, to fit.

How hard it is to adjust depends on what you expect. Some parents expect a baby to wake a few times each night to be fed. It's never easy to adjust to new sleep patterns. Parents often feel tired themselves. But they still take it in their stride and adapt around that pattern. Things can be harder for parents who expect their baby to allow them peaceful evenings and a full night's sleep. Such parents don't try to learn how to make things as easy for themselves as they can. Instead they are always frustrated.

There are some ways parents can affect a baby's sleep. You can help settle her down to bed. And you can help her learn that nighttime is for sleep. But you cannot affect the total amount of time your child sleeps. The key is to accept your baby's basic sleep needs. Then try to fit in as much sleep for yourself as you can.

HOW MUCH SLEEP DOES A BABY NEED?

The short answer is your baby needs just the amount of sleep she is getting. She will sleep neither less nor more than she needs. If you are lucky, your baby will sleep enough for you to get enough rest, too. But you might have the bad luck to find that your baby needs very little sleep at all. As a newborn, your baby may sleep as little as eight hours a day or as much as 16 or 20. As she grows, her need for sleep will change, both in total amount and in when she sleeps. She may sleep less as she goes through the first year or so. But the range of "normal" varies so much that there is no point talking about what to expect "on average." Your baby is not an average, but a unique person.

WHERE SHOULD A BABY SLEEP?

A young baby adapts well. She doesn't need one special place to sleep. The room should be warm enough for comfort, without drafts. A cradle or basket is easy to move and a good size for a young baby. A crib is a little large for a young baby. If you want to use a crib, she will feel more secure if you lie her with her head near or touching one end. You can use a crib bumper to enclose the space a bit. A baby should not have a pillow.

At night, you could have your baby in bed with you. You might find your baby sleeps better in your bed. Night feedings are easy if you are breastfeeding. And it is restful for you all. It is safe to have your baby in your bed. You will be aware of her and will not roll on her. But if you or your partner are on drugs or have been drinking, do not bring her into your bed.

All children differ in how much sleep they need. You cannot change your baby's own need for sleep. But there are ways you can affect his sleep pattern to fit your routine better.

You can let your baby sleep in a crib beside your bed. Then it's easy to deal with her at night. Or use a combination—let her sleep in your bed or beside your bed, as it suits you.

"Her sleep is perfect. She has her last feeding around seven at night. Then she'll sleep through to the next morning around seven. I often come in around half past seven and she's awake. She'll just be lying there, content, thinking I'm coming, with a big smile on her face." HELEN

Many parents like to move their babies into a separate room after a few weeks. By then, the sleeping spells at night often grow longer. But for some, a separate room right from the start is a good choice. If you are a light sleeper, you may wake at every little murmur. Or you may not be able to get back to sleep after a feeding as you listen to your baby's rustles and breathing. It is better for some parents to put the baby in a nearby room for the night.

All children differ in how much sleep they require. You cannot change your baby's own need for sleep. But there are ways you can affect his sleep pattern to fit in better with your routine.

In the daytime in warm (not hot) weather, your baby can sleep outside. Make sure she is not in direct sun. And she should be where the air circulates well. Put a mosquito net over the stroller or basket.

CHANGING SLEEP PATTERNS

Babies differ in their need for sleep. Don't blame yourself if your baby doesn't seem to sleep much. You're not doing something wrong. It's just the way she is.

Birth to six months

In the first few days of life, your baby may sleep quite a bit. Or she may take many short naps. After feeding is established, she may fall into a rhythm of sleeping and feeding. She may tend to sleep until she wakes up hungry, every two to four hours. But babies who require less sleep may wake before they are hungry. Or they may stay awake after feedings rather than dropping off when their bellies are full.

Young babies often sleep through background noise. Let normal household noise continue rather than get your baby used to complete silence for sleeping. She may always wake at a sudden noise, such as a shout or a door banging.

At first, she will have no sense of day and night. She may be as wakeful at night as during the day. Keep the room dark at night. Stay quiet and settle her back into bed as quickly as you can. She will soon learn to contrast night-time with the routines of day. Then she'll begin to have more of her wakeful hours in the day and to sleep at night.

This doesn't mean she'll sleep *through* the night, though. At three months, most babies are still awake for some time during the night. This can continue for a few more months.

Six to 12 months

Your baby is now more active and involved in the world around her. She doesn't want to be away from you. So she may begin to protest at going to bed even when she is tired. Settle her calmly with a regular routine. Then she may cry for just a few minutes when you put her to bed.

Don't leave her to cry if she is really upset. You will soon learn to tell a real cry from a grumpy protest that will fade away. When she can sit up or pull herself up to stand, she may need more help to get settled again once she is ready to go to sleep. If you go in, don't pick her up right away. Just lay her down and stroke her soothingly. Then gently but firmly let her know it is time to sleep.

There is less deep sleep now. She may wake at times, make small noises and squirm before she settles again. An intercom that transmits to you each little mutter can do more harm than good. Don't go to her when she is at this stage. Wait until she is fully awake. Otherwise you will train her to keep waking and wanting attention at frequent intervals. Instead, wait and see if she settles again by herself.

Leave some toys and board books at the foot of your baby's crib. When she wakes, she may play by herself for some time.

From three to six months, your baby may spend more time awake. He will not just wake to be fed. While he is awake, he is learning about the world around him. He may amuse himself for a short time by looking at things around him, reaching and touching. A crib mobile or toys above his crib may interest him. He may not cry for you as soon as he wakes up.

Twelve to 18 months

By now your baby may be sleeping less during the day. Perhaps she may have settled on one long midday nap. An established routine will come in handy now. A soothing cuddle, lullaby and tucking in are clear signals that it's time to go to sleep. About one baby in five still wakes during the night. But many will sleep through and wake only at times of stress, such as when ill or teething. When she wakes, she may not cry at all. Instead, she may call you and wait for you to appear.

A ROUTINE LIFE?

Having a routine for your days with your baby can be useful. You will arrange a lot of your life around when your baby needs to sleep. Rather than try to impose a routine, take your cue from your baby. There will be patterns in her waking and sleeping. Keep track for a few days. You may find it is more regular than you thought. Plan shopping, visits to friends and chores around or during sleep times.

Very young babies don't care where they are. Routines don't matter much, either. It's easy for her to sleep somewhere else if you go out for the evening. As she gets older, though, she becomes more fixed on her own routine. She may find it harder to settle down and sleep away from home. Set up your schedule so she is at home to sleep. This helps you all have a more regular and peaceful life. It may be the best approach at this time.

There are two problems with living by a baby's routine. One is that it doesn't stay the same. No sooner have you gotten used to it than it shifts.

" *Things were fine until Brian got a viral infection at seven months. For weeks, he had a fever at night. He woke up a lot. And sometimes we had to wake him to give him plenty of fluids. That set a pattern. When he was over the infection, he kept waking a lot. It only stopped when we moved him out of his crib into a bed with the sides up. That seemed to break the pattern.* " RANDY

Remain flexible. If you can change your own schedule, it will save you frustration.

The other problem with a routine is that it can become too confining. You have other interests and duties that may not fit in. You may need to go out and your baby isn't awake yet. Or perhaps her long afternoon nap means she is wide awake in the evening. And you would rather she went to bed sooner to leave you some free time. You don't have to be a slave to your baby's routine. You can expect her to be a bit flexible, too.

It's all right to wake your baby a bit early from her sleep. She may be close to waking up anyway. She may be grumpy for a little while, so allow plenty of time to wake her gently. If you want to change the time she takes a nap, try moving other parts of her day around. You could give her lunch sooner, to move the afteroon nap ahead. Being outside often keeps a baby awake. She may be ready for sleep when she comes back inside. You could try taking her out as a way of changing her nap pattern.

SETTLE YOUR BABY TO SLEEP

As soon as you notice your baby is tired, it's time to settle him to sleep. If you wait longer, he may become too tired and get upset. Then it can be harder for him to fall asleep. First be sure that all his physical needs are met. He shouldn't be hungry or thirsty. His diaper should be clean. He should be neither too hot nor cold. Then, a calm, fairly quiet place will help him wind down to sleep.

Young babies often fall asleep during a feeding. Then you can just lay him down. But don't let him become used to falling asleep at the breast or bottle. This can cause trouble later. If he will go to sleep only during a feeding, when he wakes during the night, he will wonder where he is. Then he'll cry for the breast or bottle again, rather than just drifting back to sleep. So it's best to let him become drowsy but still be awake when he's put to bed.

Soothing to sleep

There are a few time-honored techniques for soothing your baby. One is to use rhythmic movement. Rock your baby in a rocking chair. Roll him back and forth in his stroller. Go for a walk with him in a sling. Walk around with him as you gently bounce up and down. Hold him as you stand and sway. Or take him for a car ride.

He may also settle better with rhythmic sound. Sing him a song. It can be anything, not just a lullaby. And he won't mind at all if you don't have a great singing voice! You might combine singing with rocking. Let both be slow and become quiet, until they nearly fade away and then stop. You can also buy soothing tapes of womb sounds. These combine the heartbeat and whooshing sounds of life before birth. These seem to work best if they are started within the first weeks of life, before he forgets. Other sounds work, too, such as a radio tuned so it is not on a station, or the motor noise of a vacuum cleaner running in a nearby room.

Objects of comfort

Your baby may have an object of comfort to which he becomes attached. This can help him sleep. Young babies often sleep well on a sheepskin. This can be placed wherever he will be put to sleep. It can help him settle down. Your baby may prefer a certain blanket or a cuddly toy. The attachment can last for years. He may not be able to sleep without it. Taking it away for washing can cause problems.

After washing, it looks and smells different. If your child has a special object of comfort, don't take it away. Wait until he outgrows wanting it, however tattered it becomes. Be sure to take it along when you are away from home. And tell babysitters about it so it isn't left out of the crib.

Some babies become attached to a pacifier and will only sleep with it in their mouths. There are problems here, too. You have to maintain a supply of clean pacifiers. You have to get up in the night to replace one that has fallen out of a baby's mouth. And it can be hard to drop the habit. Some babies, though, have a great desire to suck. They are only satisfied and sleepy with something in their mouths. You will have to weigh the pros and cons for your baby.

Many young babies like to be swaddled before being laid down to sleep. It seems to help them feel more secure. Use a soft cloth or shawl to enclose legs and body, but leave arms free. After a few weeks, your baby will want her legs free to move during sleep. But at first it can ease falling asleep.

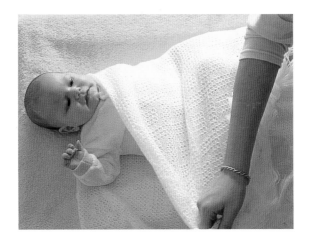

Some babies fall asleep and rest better while cuddling an object of comfort. You can't predict whether your baby will make such an attachment, or what object she may choose. But whether it's a lovely soft toy or a tattered piece of blanket, it means a lot to her.

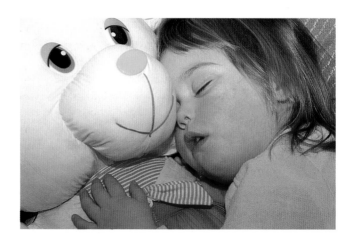

Other babies learn early—sometimes even in the womb—to suck their thumbs or fingers. This can be a soothing habit and they can control it themselves. But this also can be a tough habit to break. That may be something you will have to face when the time comes.

Positions for sleeping

A young baby should be placed on his side or back when laid down to sleep. If you lay him on his side, put his lower arm forward to stop him from rolling forward. Don't worry that he may be sick and choke if he is on his back. There is no evidence that this happens. And he will turn his head to one side in any case.

Research about sudden infant death shows that it is more common among babies who sleep on their stomachs. So, for a young baby, it is best not to put him down on his stomach. By the time he is old enough to turn over by himself, it is safe to let him sleep in any position he prefers.

NIGHTTIME

An evening routine that marks the change from daytime can help make nights more peaceful. You might start with a bath. Then cuddle in a quiet room and look at a book together. Then follow with a last feeding.

Wakeful baby

A young baby who is awake at night for more than a quick feeding will have tired parents. The baby himself will not be tired. He may not need more sleep. He may want company during the night, instead. If you have a wakeful baby, try bringing your baby into your bed. He may be calmed by your presence and you may get more sleep.

Because your baby is fine, just work on how *you* can manage. Rest when you can in the day. And go to bed early. But daytime rest won't make up for broken nights. So share the load with your partner. Your partner may have to get up for work in the morning. But so do you. If you are breast-feeding, express and store some milk. Then the father can give a nighttime bottle of breast milk while you get a little more sleep. He can also let you sleep in now and then. If you are bottle-feeding, you can take turns with night feedings. Or you can have alternate nights on duty. Losing sleep with a baby is never easy. But having enough support can keep you from sinking into constant fatigue or depression.

Waking for feedings

Some babies keep on waking up during the night, long after they are on solid foods. And one baby in five still wakes through the second year of life.

You could try leaving him for a few minutes when he wakes to see if he will go back to sleep. If you want to try to change the waking habit, when you go to him, don't give him milk or juice. Just give him plain water or nothing at all. Touch him as little as you can. And settle him firmly back to bed as soon as you can.

If you have been nursing him or giving him a bottle, this will seem like a big shift to him. And he is likely to protest. It might help to warn him. Even at less than one year old, your baby will understand some of what you say to him, as well as your tone of voice. Tell him firmly as you settle him for sleep,

TIPS FOR SLEEP

- *If you lay your baby to sleep on her side, be sure her ear is flat. And keep changing which side you lay her on.*
- *Warm up the crib with a hot water bottle. This can help your baby get to sleep. But take it out before you put your baby down.*
- *Don't let your baby fall asleep with a bottle. Saliva slows down in sleep so the milk isn't rinsed away. It can cause new teeth to decay. Sweet drinks are even worse.*
- *It's harmful for a baby to be too warm while sleeping. Use a few light blankets that you can add or take away. Don't use quilts or baby sleeping bags. Don't overdress your baby for sleep, either. And the room should be just warm enough for you.*
- *If you are doing chores while your baby sleeps, stop and rest for 15 minutes before you think he may wake up.*
- *Allow extra time for settling your baby to sleep when you are going out. He'll know if you are trying to rush things and won't settle down.*

"No crying at night. No milk at night. Night is for sleeping." When he wakes at night, repeat this as you calmly but firmly tuck him in.

If one parent normally handles the night wakings and feedings, it may help for the other parent to go instead. Then your baby won't expect milk and will know that something has changed. A few nights of this routine may be enough to convince a baby that it's not worth it to wake up.

Be consistent if you decide to make this change. If you give in and offer a feeding and cuddle, you will have undone the lesson. If your baby is upset by the change and cries for you, it will be very stressful to listen to. You need your partner's support. Or ask a friend to come spend a few nights to give you moral support.

A routine will comfort both you and your baby. Leave him for five minutes. Then you or your partner can go in and repeat the message that it's time to go to sleep. Leave again, for a few minutes longer this time. Repeat this pattern until your baby learns that he has nothing to gain from crying and falls asleep. Often a night or two of this is all that is needed. Then you can all enjoy very welcome nights of unbroken sleep.

When your baby wakes at night, take care of him quietly in subdued light. Interact as little as you can. There should be no sociable reward for being awake at night. Soon your baby will learn that night is for sleeping. Then you can both get back to sleep quickly.

QUESTIONS AND ANSWERS

Q: At three months, my baby had been waking only once or twice a night for a feeding. But suddenly she is waking every couple of hours. Does this mean breast milk isn't enough and she needs to start on solids?

A: No, she doesn't need to start solids yet. Four months is the soonest to begin solid foods, and six months is better. Your baby may be in a growing spurt. Growing spurts often come at around six weeks, three months and four-and-a-half months. A breast-fed baby will need more frequent feedings at these times for a few days. This will soon build up the milk supply. So stick with it. Your baby should soon go back to sleeping for longer periods.

Q: At six in the morning, my baby is awake and ready for action. I'd really like to sleep another hour. Any suggestions?

A: A mobile or toys tied to a piece of elastic over the crib might keep your baby busy for a while. Put him to sleep on his back so he can see them when he wakes. A dim light in the room would also help on dark mornings. When he fusses for a feeding, bring him into your bed. You can doze a bit afterwards. Once he is able to sit up, leave board books and toys in the crib. These can keep him busy for a while. Change the toys, mobiles or books every few days. He will have more interest in things that are new. Wakeful babies are often bright and curious. They can be quite happy playing by themselves.

Q: My baby sleeps in a crib next to my bed. Sometimes in the night I hear his breathing stop for a few seconds. When he's been sleeping longer than I expect, I have to go and check that he's still breathing. What can I do to protect him from sudden infant death syndrome?

A: Every parent knows the fear that their baby may simply stop breathing in the night. It's made worse by the fact that we don't know all the causes of crib death and so we can't always prevent it. It can occur at any age up to 18 months or so. But it happens most often between birth and five months. Luckily it is rare. And there are simple steps you can take to reduce the risk. Try not to think too much about it and become too anxious. It is normal for a baby up to three months to have a breathing pattern of light panting followed by a pause that lasts a few seconds. Comfort yourself by putting a hand on your baby if you are worried.

Make sure to get your baby used to sleeping on his side or back rather than on his stomach. He shouldn't get hot in his sleep from too warm a room or too many clothes or covers. A smoke-free home lowers the risk, so ask any smokers to step outside. If your baby has a cold or other infection, see your doctor. Be very careful about overheating. Some worry is natural. But if you find yourself very anxious, talk to your doctor.

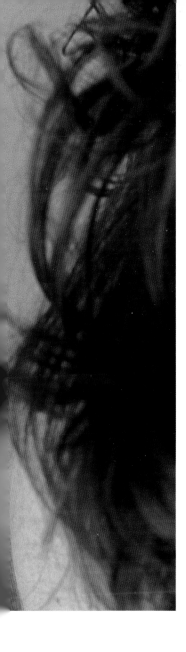

7

Crying

" I've never been able to let her scream without picking her up. When babies are tiny, you feel you have to do something to comfort them. Even when nothing I did helped, I kept thinking to myself this can only go on for so long. "

CRYING TO COMMUNICATE

"How can there be a baby with no crying?" asks an old folk song. We all know babies and crying go together. But if a baby's cry is a normal part of life, why does it have the power to drive parents crazy like no other sound?

It's all part of nature's plan for human survival. You are meant to have a strong response to your baby's cry. If it didn't trigger you to action, your baby might not have crucial needs met. And his survival might be in question.

Crying is a new baby's only way to tell you that something is wrong. He doesn't know what the problem is. But he knows he doesn't feel well or he's in pain right now. So he expresses how he feels. It will be weeks and months before he learns the difference between feeling hungry, or cold, or lonely. It also takes time to learn that you can and will help him. As he finds other ways to express himself, he will rely less on crying. How you respond to his cries from the start is part of the process of teaching him to trust. He will come to learn that he will be all right. You will respond to him. And he doesn't have to cry so much.

Follow your instincts

Within a few days of your baby's birth, you will recognize his cry. Your urge will be to do something to get the crying to stop. This urge comes partly from tender concern for your baby's well-being. But the instinct to help him is more than that. A chemical change in your body also spurs you into action. Your baby's cry is a powerful force. It causes stress hormones to be released into your bloodstream. They increase your blood pressure, breathing rate and muscle tension. This feels upsetting. The more the crying goes on, the worse you feel. You must do something. And if the crying doesn't stop, you may end up feeling frantic and in tears yourself.

Your strong instinct is to try to find the cause of your baby's crying. You want to make things right and have him calm and peaceful again. This is what makes you feel good. And it is just the response your baby needs. He wants you to help him when he cries. He needs to learn that the world is a good place to be. And he needs to begin to trust in life and in you.

Spoiling the child?

If you do follow your instincts and pick up your baby when he cries, you may hear that you are "spoiling" him. But leaving a baby to cry doesn't keep him from crying. If he is left, he becomes more unhappy. And so he cries more. He becomes frantic and insecure. He learns to expect that no help will come when he needs it. As he grows older, he doesn't feel content and confident, but keeps on fussing and crying.

Her parents will learn to tune into her needs and her other signals. She makes sucking noises or roots around with her mouth as a sign of hunger. She rubs her eyes to signal fatigue. She may begin to cry less as her needs are met before she has to complain.

One study found that babies whose mothers respond quickly, when they cry in the first three months of life, cry less often. They also cry for less time than those whose mothers delay or ignore crying. By four months, the promptly seen-to babies are less likely to keep crying. And at one year of age, they are more independent. They can also express themselves in more ways other than crying.

From baby to toddler

A young baby cries to express the needs he feels at the moment. Those needs are frequent. To him, they feel strange and intense. He needs to be fed and changed. He gets tired or too tense. He needs to be touched and held. He has much to adjust to all at once in the sudden change from life in the womb. It makes sense that he may cry quite often. He cries most when he cannot see, hear or touch his mother. The best way to settle him down in the early weeks is to pick him up and feed him.

By about four months, he may cry less than before. Now he can express himself in other ways as he smiles and laughs with his parents. A rhythm of care begins to build. And learning each other's signals means he has less need to cry.

66When she was a few weeks old, she had a pattern of crying for about a half-hour every evening. I'd just let her cry. It just seemed she needed a crying time. And it wasn't bad crying. It stopped and started. Now she can see more things out the the window and on the wall and she's more content. 99 HEATHER

66*He went through a phase at 16 months of screaming at night. He would keep us up all night. My sister said, 'You'll just have to leave him.' So I lay on the floor of his room where he could see me and put cotton balls in my ears. He screamed for an hour and 15 minutes and then went to sleep. He cried less the next night. And then it stopped. Being in his room but not doing anything, he knew where I was. And I could see he wasn't hitting his head against the crib so it gave me some comfort.* 99 JANE

When he is eight months old, his crying spells are less frequent. Often they are clearly linked to events around him. It may frustrate him that he wants to do something he can't quite manage. He may be bored and cry because he wants company. Or he may cry from fear when a stranger picks him up.

Between a year and 18 months, he develops a much bigger range of ways to express himself. So he relies less on crying. He can use a few words and meaningful sounds. He points or uses other gestures. And he shows his feelings in his face. But he will still cry when something frustrates him. It upsets him when he cannot yet do something he wants to do. And he doesn't like to be told "no." He will also cry when you leave him.

WHY IS YOUR BABY CRYING?

Babies cry because something is wrong and they feel unhappy. Learn your baby's signals and respond promptly to her needs. That's how you can help her to become happy and confident about life.

Hunger

For a young baby, hunger is new and unpleasant. It feels urgent. By the time she is a few months old, your baby can be more patient if she knows food is coming. An older baby or toddler has a less-urgent appetite. But he will still be fretful and demanding when hungry.

What to do: Feeding a young baby is the best way to settle her down. If you are breast-feeding, offer the breast first when she cries. If she is not hungry, she may not nurse. Or she may nurse more for comfort than food. Don't worry about nursing too much. She may take just the less-filling foremilk. If you are bottle-feeding, you can still offer a feeding. But you have to be more careful. You don't want to feed her too much. If your baby has recently had a feeding, you could still offer a little more milk to help her settle down. But don't let her take a whole bottle.

Don't delay feeding your baby when she is hungry. She may become more upset. Then it can be tough to settle her down for a feeding when you are ready. If she is frantic, she may swallow too much air with her feeding. This can cause her to throw up or get a stomachache. Try to stop or at least reduce the crying before a feeding. She may calm down for a bit if you rock her or bounce her gently up and down. Pat her back and talk to her as you get ready to feed her.

Need for contact

Your baby's need for contact with a loving caretaker is immense. She may cry because she can't see or hear you. Or she may need to be held and feel the comfort of your presence. She is not trying to control you. She is just expressing a real need.

What to do: Pick her up. Being held may be all she needs. You can get used to doing all sorts of chores with one arm. Or try a baby sling. With a sling she is in contact with you and you still have both arms free to do your work.

Too much excitement

It's easy for a baby to become overwhelmed by all the sights and sounds around them. Even being talked to, looked at, held and rocked can be too much at times. A young baby cannot tune things out, so she can become tense and stressed. At times like this, the more you do to settle down your baby, the worse it can get. This often happens toward the end of the day. You may notice your baby's body stiffen. She may push out with arms and legs. And she may cry more when you pick her up.

What to do: Calm things down around your baby. Darken the room. Don't make eye contact with her or speak. Use only low sounds, like a "shhhh, shhhh" or a low hum. Lay her down, rather than holding or rocking her. And if you touch her at all, just place a quiet hand on her. Swaddling (see page 91) may help because it limits movement and keeps her still. But she may fight it at first. She may need to cry for a few minutes to release tension. So leave her for a few minutes to see if she winds down.

Your baby needs a lot of physical contact with you. But sometimes even being held is tiring and can frazzle a baby's nerves. You need to decide whether contact like holding and rocking is helping or stillness is needed.

Discomfort

Lots of things may bother your baby. Clothes may pull. He can be too hot or cold. He can have gas, be teething, or need a diaper change. No one knows if babies really mind being wet. One study found that babies who were picked up, changed, and had the same wet diaper put back on, seemed just as happy as those who were given a dry diaper. Perhaps being handled was more important than being dry. A soiled diaper can irritate your baby's skin, though, and may make your baby cry.

What to do: Try to find the problem, and fix it. If you can't tell what's wrong, start trying things to learn what might help. For teething, a ring to chew on that has been chilled in the refrigerator is soothing.

Illness or pain

A cry of pain is often abrupt. It can be a loud cry followed by a silence as the baby draws breath to let out a scream. A loud, intense wail with knees drawn up may suggest the baby has colic. Colic may be caused by painful cramps in the bowel (see page 105). The cry of a baby who is ill may be less intense, low and moaning.

What to do: If you can see what's causing pain, deal with it and soothe your baby. If your baby's cry doesn't sound right, she may be getting ill. Contact your doctor.

Boredom

The need to learn and to be social is very strong. Your baby may cry if she is lonely or bored.

SOOTHING A CRYING BABY

- *First pick her up and try feeding her.*
- *Walk around with her up on your shoulder. Walk with a rhythmic dip in your step just when she takes a big breath in for another cry.*
- *Keep your movements calm and regular. Don't bounce or jiggle.*
- *Put her in a sling and go for a walk.*
- *Swaddle her so she feels snug and secure.*
- *Keep humming or singing. Or play music for her.*
- *Rock her in a rocking chair, with a shawl wrapped around you both.*
- *Lay her down and rub or pat her back.*
- *Take her for a ride in the car.*
- *Have a bath together. Follow with a gentle massage.*
- *Try a pacifier if she is calmed by sucking.*

Sucking often brings comfort even when it has nothing to do with a feeding. Babies may suck their fingers or thumbs, or a pacifier. A breast-fed baby may find comfort by sucking at the breast, even after a feeding when he is not hungry.

What to do: Don't expect your baby to lie calmly just because she is fed and her diaper is dry. Put a clean quilt on the floor. Put her down on her belly on the quilt with some colorful toys. Then let her creep around and explore. Or put her in an infant seat where she can see you. Take her outside. Hang toys where she can see and reach them. With an older baby, let her play near you. Include her in what you are doing. Her attention span with objects may be short. But if you get involved too, from time to time, she will be more involved as well.

Frustration

Babies have a huge drive to do things. It can frustrate a baby to try to do something he cannot yet do. Being told "no" can also frustrate him and can lead to tears.

What to do: Tactful help and support at the right time can prevent upsets. Hold the toy in place that keeps falling over. Or move something within her reach. If she keeps crying because she can't do something, try to

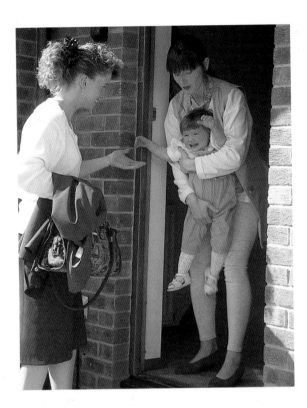

Crying when you leave is a sign your baby is growing. She has learned how important and special you are to her. It may help if you prepare her. But be patient. This is a normal stage.

distract her. Show her something new. Distract her instead of telling her "no." It also helps prevent problems if you childproof your house.

Separation

Before about four months, your baby will not cry if you leave her with someone else. But as she grows, she learns to tell her trusted people from strangers. Then she may cry if you go away from her. At certain stages, especially when she is learning new skills, she will become more clinging.

What to do: Try not to leave your baby with strangers. Let her get to know people while you are there before she is left with them. Don't force her to go to someone when she doesn't want to. When you leave her, let her know you are going and that you will be back. An older baby or toddler can understand the meaning of "back." Don't sneak out. That will only make her more nervous about separation. Be patient when she needs to feel secure. In the long run, it will help make things easier.

STILL CRYING?

You may have found the problem and dealt with it. But your baby is still crying. Now what? Sometimes your baby can be so worked up that he can't stop crying. It's as if being upset upsets him! Then it's time to try soothing techniques that may help him unwind. Don't give up when one technique doesn't work. Just try another. You may feel worked up yourself by the crying, so take some deep breaths and try to calm yourself. If you are tense and upset, your baby will feel it and become even more stressed. Luckily, a lot of the soothing techniques, like rocking and singing, will calm you, too.

If nothing seems to help, ask your partner or someone else to take over. Often someone who is less involved will be more calm and your baby may settle down. It will also give you a break. If no one else is there, put your baby down in a safe place. Then close the door and leave him. Walk around your yard. Make yourself a cup of fragrant tea. Or just sit down and breathe deeply. Your baby will be OK. He may settle down in a few minutes. If not, at least *you* will be calmer. You'll be more able to help him when you go back.

COLIC

No one knows for sure what causes colic or how to prevent it. It often begins at around three weeks and stops at around three months. Your baby may have crying spells that can last for hours. They occur most often in the evenings. The baby seems to be in intense pain as he screams, draws up his knees and often passes gas. Except for this, the baby seems to thrive and be healthy.

One thought is that colic is caused by a spasm in the baby's bowel. The baby may be sensitive to certain foods. For breast-feeding mothers, try removing things from your diet. Don't eat chocolate, cabbage, onions, green peppers or any milk products or butter for at least a week. For bottle-fed babies, talk with your doctor. A change of formula might help. If the colic improves or goes away, stick to the changes you made.

Some people think the problem isn't caused by food. The crying may tend to come at one time of day and not after feedings. It may be caused by tension. This would explain why the most common time for colic is evening, when you and your baby are both most tired. You could give your baby a calming bath or massage in the afternoon to release tension. Or take him out for a walk. Prepare dinner early in the day so there is no pressure later. Have a good lunch. Rest in the afternoon if you can. Use soothing techniques with your baby. And make sure to keep all your movements relaxed and slow rather than bouncing.

A matter of weeks seems like ages when your baby is crying. But at least colic often stops abruptly. It really is brief compared with all the time and pleasure you will share with your baby.

From six in the evening until midnight, she'd cry, nurse and nurse, throw up, then nurse again. She always struggled at the breast. It was awful, just what you don't need at the end of the day. We tried medicines, but nothing worked. Then suddenly she stopped. PATTY

CRYING . . . AND CRYING

Some babies cry more than most, no matter what you do. It may look like colic, but it may not come at a certain time of day. And it may last beyond the time when colic often stops. Parents usually get a lot of advice. And they will try one thing after another. But nothing seems to help. They may feel that they are no good as parents. They may feel angry at the baby. And they can feel guilty for feeling angry.

There is no magic answer to the problem. But it helps to know that it is not your fault. You are not doing something wrong. It isn't your baby's fault, either. Some babies just have a harder time at first than others. In the early weeks, the type of labor and drugs used can affect a baby's level of tension. If the mother suffered high levels of stress in pregnancy, the baby may be more likely to cry. Long exposure to the mother's stress hormones might leave the baby keyed up. It takes time for the tension to be released. No matter what the reason, some babies are more touchy than others and cry more.

Do what you can to get through this time. But don't wear yourselves out trying one thing after another. Find support for yourself. Share with a partner. Get help for an hour or so to get out and have a break. Talk things over with a friend to relieve your stress. Your doctor may be a source of support. A self-help group for parents of crying babies might help. The Friends' Health Connection may also provide support (see Appendix).

It's normal to feel unsure of yourself. You may worry that you are doing something wrong when your baby keeps on crying. But don't blame yourself or your baby. Give yourself credit for coping. And give yourself a break when you can.

QUESTIONS AND ANSWERS

Q: How can I tell what my baby wants when she cries?
A: A new baby's cry doesn't vary much. But she will learn that you come when she cries. Then it will become more as if she is calling you. You'll know when she gives a really frantic cry of urgent hunger or pain, or a grumpy, tired cry. There are other clues as well. Check the look on her face. Is her body tense or relaxed? How is she breathing? You will also know her routine. That will give you some clues as to why she is crying. As you tune into her, you will be able to make a good guess about her message.

Q: Last night my baby wouldn't stop crying. I was so tired myself that all at once I just couldn't stand it. If my husband hadn't been there, I don't know what I would have done. Am I a terrible mother?
A: Your baby's crying upsets you a great deal. You may feel ready to snap when it doesn't stop. Most parents feel they reach the breaking point now and then. So don't blame yourself. But you must recognize the feeling. Then you can get help or take a break before you lash out at your baby.

If you feel angry at your baby's crying, it's time to put him down safely and take a break. You can't calm him when you are upset and angry yourself. Hand him over to your partner, if you can. Or call a friend or go to a neighbor. If there is nobody you can go to, get away from your baby's crying until you calm down. Listen to music with headphones. Or have a bath with your ears under water.

If you fear that you could hurt your baby, it's time to get help. Call your doctor or the National Child Abuse Hotline (see Appendix) for support. You need help and support to deal with the strain. And you need a safety valve for when everything is just too much.

Q: When my baby was little, I never left her crying for long. But now she's 15 months old. She's begun to whine and cry for attention. If I comfort her now when she cries, won't she make a habit of it?
A: With older babies, it is true that crying becomes a less-instant way to express needs. But it's still a way to get her message across. At 15 months, your daughter does need a lot of attention. Her own attention span is short. She may get bored and need you to play with her. She may need you to get her involved with toys. Then she can play by herself for a little while. The problem is not so much that she's asking for attention. It's just that the way she asks is upsetting.

Don't ignore her crying for very long. When you do give her your attention, she will learn that if she just keeps it up long enough it will work. Instead, try to take the focus off the crying. Don't offer cuddles and sympathy. Be more matter-of-fact. Distract her from crying with something else. Talk to her about what you and she are doing. Put words to what you think she is asking. And respond to other signals she gives. Then she will learn that crying is not the only way, nor the best way, to get your attention.

8

On to Solids

" At five months, Karen was ready to start solids. She'd been sitting on my lap while I had my meal. She'd watch every bite from my plate to my mouth. One day she grabbed some. So I gave her a nibble and she ate it right up. It was really easy to just let her have a taste of what we were having. "

TIME TO WEAN

Milk is the perfect food for your young baby. But after a while, the breast or bottle is no longer enough. It becomes time to slowly switch to eating a wide range of foods. Milk will still be your baby's main food and source of nourishment for months after starting solid foods. But certain changes in your baby show she's ready for a change.

Just when that point arrives won't be the same from one baby to the next. Between four and six months is often the best time. At three months or before, your baby's system is not yet able to digest foods other than milk. Foods given at this early stage may cause allergic reactions. After four months, your baby's gut will be able to cope with solids. Allergies are less likely when foods are chosen and offered with care.

After six months, there are good reasons why your baby needs solid food. Milk contains little iron. Your baby prepared for this before birth by storing enough iron in her liver to last her through the first few months. But by around six months, her iron stores begin to run low. Then she needs the iron that solid foods can provide.

There will be other signs that she is ready to start solids. Can she sit up with support and not fall sideways? Are teeth starting to emerge? Even without back teeth, your baby likes to gnaw and chew on things with her strong gums. By about six months, she can use her tongue to move food to the back of her mouth. She no longer just sticks out her tongue and pushes out food with it. She will begin to put things into her own mouth. And she will have an active interest in the foods you eat.

Wait until around six months to start solids if your baby shows no real need or desire before then. At six months, you skip the messy stage of feeding tiny amounts of nearly liquid food to a baby who spits most of it back at you. By about six months, your baby can swallow more firmly textured food. She can also manage some finger foods. After the sixth month, she will move more quickly to family food.

FIRST FOODS

There are many good choices for your baby's first foods. She will be taking only small amounts to start with. You'll want to start with foods that are easy to prepare as well as good for her. A dry baby cereal mixed with a little breast milk or formula makes a good start. Use rice cereal rather than wheat or oats. Rice contains no gluten, which some babies are allergic to. You can also try cooked and puréed vegetables such as yams, sweet potatoes or carrots. Stewed and puréed apple or pear or mashed very ripe banana or avocado also work well.

Whatever you choose, it's wise to try just one food at a time. This way you will know which food is a problem if your baby has any adverse reaction. Breakfast or lunch are good times to begin solids. Your baby will be alert. And

Food is fun. By the time your baby is ready for solids, he will delight in new tastes and textures. He will also want to be involved in the process of eating. Let him try to use his own spoon even if he can't manage it well.

you will be able to keep an eye on her for the rest of the day. After two or three days of offering some of the first food, you can try another.

Prevent reactions

Some foods are more likely than others to disagree with your baby. Some may cause an allergic reaction. Others may just be hard to digest. Leave such foods for later, when your baby is older and has been eating solid foods for some time. Then try them one at a time and watch out for any reaction. These signs can mean your baby is not able to handle a food:

- rash
- vomiting
- asthma
- swelling lips
- colic
- sore bottom
- eczema

If any of these signs appear after starting a new food, leave it out for a few weeks. Then try it again. These foods are most likely to cause adverse reactions:

- wheat
- egg
- chocolate
- strawberries
- citrus fruits
- mushrooms
- shellfish

Prepared baby foods are an easy choice when you are away from home. They don't have to be heated if your baby likes them as they are. If you feed your baby right from the jar, throw out any leftovers.

Eggs can be an great source of protein and minerals for your baby. But at first give her only the yolk. The yolk is less likely to cause a reaction than egg white. If there is no problem with yolks, try egg whites later. If your baby refuses egg or vomits after eating it, wait two months before you try it again.

READY-MADE OR HOMEMADE

There are benefits to both homemade and ready-made baby foods. Many parents use both. When you make your baby's food yourself, you can use fresh foods with the highest food values. Your baby will get used to home cooking right from the start. He will get used to more tastes and textures than those in ready-made foods. And it can be simpler to move him over to family meals. It may also be cheaper to make the food yourself. Buy fruits and vegetables in season. A blender or food processor is all you need to make purées.

Ready-made baby food is simpler to use. It limits waste because you just open small amounts at a time. Additives and preservatives are limited in baby foods. Ingredients are also screened for pesticide levels. Read the labels so you know just what your baby is getting. They will be listed in order of how much is present in the food. Single fruits and vegetables have more food value than mixed dinners, which may be mostly starchy cereal. Single foods give you more control over starting foods one at a time.

❝ *I've started her at four months with whole-grain toast mixed with banana. She'll have that for a month or so before I give her a little oatmeal in the morning. By about six months, I think her daily routine will fit in with ours. Then it will be simpler.* **❞** RACHEL

No-sugar-added baby foods and drinks are on the market. But check labels. And watch out for sugar listed under other names, such as maltose, dextrose, glucose or fructose.

Sometimes adults are fooled into buying baby foods that sound good to adult tastes. But it makes much more sense to think about nutrition first. In any case, your baby will likely prefer simple flavors.

MAKING EARLY MEALS

By the time your baby is ready for solids, you won't have to sterilize the things you use. Wash all utensils in hot water, as you do for the rest of the family. And use basic food hygiene. Wash your hands well before you begin. And wash all fruits and vegetables before using them. This will help ensure safety. If you are using ready-made baby food, don't feed right from the jar. If your baby eats only some of it, you might want to save the rest for later. Instead, spoon the part you expect him to eat into another dish.

Homemade food should be made without added salt. Before the age of eight months or so, your baby's kidneys won't be able to cope with excess salt. If you plan to use some of the food cooked for the family, cook without salt. Let others add it at the table if they wish.

Purée your baby's first foods in a blender or processor. Then push through a sieve to make sure it is smooth. Remove any pulp or tough skins from fruits or vegetables. Stew fruits such as apples, pears, peaches or apricots in a little water before blending. Once your baby gets used to cooked fruit, you can serve fresh apple by scraping the sharp edge of a spoon across the apple flesh, until it is all scraped into a mush.

Liquify homemade food for your baby, and freeze some for later use. It works well to freeze the food in ice-cube trays. Then store the cubes in plastic bags in the freezer to thaw later or warm in baby-size servings.

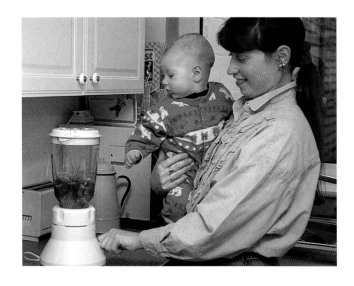

You may want to make more food than he will want at one time. So you might like to freeze food for your baby. To reduce the risks from germs, cool cooked food quickly in the refrigerator. Then freeze it as soon as it is chilled. Frozen fruits and vegetables just need to be thawed well before serving. Warm them if you like. Don't freeze foods with meat or fish. They must be reheated completely by boiling before they are safe to feed your baby. And the small amounts you will be using are likely to stick to the pan and burn.

Early food should be fairly liquid. Add water or milk as needed. As your baby becomes used to solids, you can leave the texture a little firmer. By six or seven months, you can simply mash most vegetables rather than straining them.

Begin with cereals, fruits and vegetables. Then you can move on to protein foods, such as cottage cheese, eggs, meat and fish. Meat and fish should be well cooked. Blend and strain it at first. But by about ten months, meat can be chopped into tiny pieces and fish can be flaked. Beans and lentils are high in protein. But make them easier to digest by cooking them well.

FROM MUSH TO MEALS

Between four and six months, milk is still your baby's main source of nourishment. But solids can boost the range of nutrients. They help satisfy hunger. And they pave the way to broader eating habits later on. You may offer solids once or twice each day, perhaps at noon and in the evening. Your baby will do better with solid food if he is not too hungry. So take the edge off his hunger by giving him breast or bottle first. Then interrupt the milk feeding to feed him solids.

At six to eight months, your baby branches out into more textures and tastes. But milk remains the center of his diet. He is able to scoop up food with his hand to feed himself. He can manage some finger foods. And he may try to use a spoon.

Between eight and 12 months, your baby may have three solid meals a day. The balance will shift so that solid foods form more of his diet than milk. Then you can start his meal with solids and finish with milk. He will now be able pick up peas and other finger foods. And he'll do fairly well with a spoon, though he'll be a little messy.

From one year to 18 months, your baby won't grow as quickly as he did before. You may be surprised to find that he wants to eat less than he did before. Don't worry. Just offer him good wholesome food. Don't give him too many cookies or sweet drinks like juice, which can fill him

"Life seems more routine now that he's having solid food. We have to get home for mealtimes or else cope with all the mess when we're out. Most of the time, it doesn't seem worth it. We just try to be home to fit his meal schedule." SHARON

Zwieback, or the homemade equivalent—strips of bread slowly toasted in the oven until dry—are popular. Bread is more likely to break off and choke a young baby, but can be a good finger food by seven months or so. Chunks of cooked carrot or potato, cubes of cheese, pieces of banana, orange segments or other soft fruits can all be given by the age of six months.

up between meals. Then he will eat what he needs to grow well and be healthy. By now, he will fit fairly well into family meals. Just chop things up well and he can mostly feed himself. He will need help when he is tired. And you may have to remind him to eat if he starts playing with his food. Use tact to support his efforts without taking over.

DRINKS

As soon as your baby is taking much solid food, offer him plain, cooled, boiled water to drink. He can begin to take drinks from a cup by five or six months. You may like to start him with a trainer cup with a spout. The drinking action is somewhere between sucking and drinking. Your baby can handle a trainer cup by himself fairly soon. A cup with two handles might be the simplest to use. Or you can go right from breast or bottle to taking some drinks from a normal cup. When you skip a trainer cup, your baby won't rely on the lid to prevent spills. And he may learn to use a normal cup on his own more quickly.

As solid meals increase, your baby will drop some milk feedings. But he may have milk along with his meals. By ten months or so, he may have breast milk or a bottle just in the morning and before bed, with three solid meals in the day. For a breast-fed baby, nursing is about much more than milk. He may like to nurse for comfort or to settle down for a nap. For most babies, the evening milk feeding is the last to go. Breast-feeding or a bottle with the closeness and cuddling it brings is enjoyed before bedtime well into or throughout the second year.

DON'T LET YOUR BABY BECOME OVERWEIGHT

For adults, being overweight or obese contributes to a number of diseases. It also causes a great deal of grief. Babies who are fat are more likely to become fat children and fat adults. This is partly because the fat storage cells, which will be there for life, are produced in the first year. Fat babies produce more of these fat cells. In later years, these fat cells are readily filled and swollen. As adults, these people find it is easier for them to gain weight and harder to lose it. So prevent your baby from becoming overweight. It's one way you can help protect his future.

To keep your baby from becoming overweight, don't start solids too soon. Don't add sugar to your baby's food. Let him feed himself as much as he can. Then he will take what he needs. He may eat too much if you spoon it in because he likes to be fed. He also won't be under pressure to have just a few more bites. Don't praise him for eating all his food. And don't be upset if he leaves something. To cut down on waste, just give him small amounts at a time. Give him more only if he has finished it and wants more.

Don't hand your baby cookies to buy a few more minutes' peace and quiet when he fusses. Cookies are fattening. They are also bad for his teeth. Give him some of your time and attention instead. This way you won't be training him to reach for food when he feels grumpy.

By 18 months, your child can eat and drink by himself fairly well. But he will still need tactful help when he is tired, grumpy or distracted. He will also choose a good diet if he is offered a range of wholesome foods.

- *Use a long, shallow weaning spoon with smooth edges for feeding your baby.*
- *Food can be served at room temperature or slightly warmed.*
- *Never give your baby popcorn or peanuts. They are very dangerous if choked on or inhaled into the lungs.*
- *Start a pattern of healthful eating right from the start. Feed your baby plenty of fruits, vegetables and whole grains. Limit sweet and fatty foods.*
- *Buy plain yogurt and add your own mashed or puréed fruit. This will provide better food value than sweetened fruit yogurts, which may also contain harmful additives.*
- *Don't use foods with additives. Some, such as colorings, may cause hyperactive behavior in some babies and children.*
- *Don't give your baby foods with small seeds, such as raspberries or grapes, or bread with wheat kernels.*
- *Milk and plain water are the best drinks for your baby. Only serve fruit juice once in a while. Sweet drinks can harm teeth even before they emerge. And coffee and tea are stimulants that block the uptake of some nutrients.*

Handy snacks don't have to be "junk" food with a lot of calories but not much else. Babies love lots of nutritious foods, such as:

- a banana
- squares of whole-wheat bread and butter
- a piece of cheese
- dried fruit
- apples, peeled and sliced

HAPPY MEALTIMES

People are social beings. We love to share a meal with others. Your baby is no exception. He will enjoy your attention and be pleased to be part of a family scene when others are present. But there are few parts of family life that bring as much trouble and worry as meals. And problems often have their roots with the first solid meals.

We can get into trouble when we put a lot of strong feelings into food. You may feel good inside when your baby eats and enjoys all the food you have made for him. But you may feel upset or even angry if he turns away from it. So you coax him and urge him. And you spend extra time trying to

sneak in one more mouthful. Then he learns that this is important to you and a sure way to get plenty of attention. The scene is set for a battle of wills that you never can win.

Stay relaxed about how much your baby eats and what he likes or rejects. A healthy baby will not starve himself. He will eat what he needs if he's given a range of healthful food. Just don't fill him up on cookies and sweet drinks between meals. If he has a chance to get hungry between meals, he will be sure to eat what he needs at mealtimes. He may have times when he turns down a food he loved the week before. Or he may stick to a certain kind of food for a while. Just let it pass. He will be learning to rely on his healthy appetite. And mealtimes can stay a happy time.

Keep relaxed about what, how much and how well your baby eats. You will all enjoy family meals more. Your baby will be able to develop a healthy appetite without getting involved in a tangle of emotions.

QUESTIONS AND ANSWERS

Q: I'm concerned about my son having a good diet. And I want to protect his teeth. Is it true that if a baby isn't given any foods with sugar added it will keep him from getting a sweet tooth?

A: Babies are drawn to sweetness. Even breast milk and bottle milk are quite sweet. So staying away from foods with added sugar won't stop your baby from liking a sweet taste. But there are different kinds of sweet foods. Fruits have a subtle sweetness along with lots of other flavor. Refined sugar gives a blast of pure sweetness. Refined sugar, unlike natural sweetness, also has a strong effect on blood-sugar levels. This can lead to cravings for more. So don't feed your baby foods with added sugar. As he gets older, you might not be able to outlaw all sweets and sugary foods. But you could limit them to mealtimes and clean his teeth afterwards.

Q: My daughter is nine months old. She still shows no interest in solid food. I've slowly started her on a range of foods. But she will only eat a spoonful or two, then she turns her face away. She seems happy just with breast milk. Will she be missing out on what she needs?

A: Not all babies are eager to try solid foods. Meanwhile, breast milk still provides good nutrition for your baby. Ask your doctor whether she might need a vitamin-and-mineral supplement. Nutrients such as iron and vitamin D are low in breast milk. Keep giving her solid food without any pressure. This will help your daughter take pleasure in a wider range of foods when she is ready. She may do well with finger foods to gnaw on. You could focus on iron-rich foods. Try egg yolk, strips of whole-grain toast or cooked beans. Pieces of fruit can contain vitamin C, which helps iron to be absorbed better, too.

Q: I am vegetarian and would like to raise my baby to be vegetarian, too. Any pointers?

A: Your baby can flourish on a vegetarian diet. Just make sure you provide complete protein in nonmeat foods. Vegetable proteins need to be combined to provide full usable protein. Serve beans such as lentils with grains as in cereal, bread, pasta or rice. You can also combine nuts with grains, or grains with dairy products. Be sure your baby can digest the food. Cook well, then grind or sieve to remove tough skins.

If you give your baby cheese, yogurt and eggs, there should be no problem in providing complete nutrition. But there are special concerns if you decide on a vegan diet with no animal products. It is hard to provide enough calcium in a vegan diet. And it's almost impossible to provide vitamin B12. Vitamin B12 is essential for the nervous system. So supplement your baby's diet with calcium and B12.

To talk with a nutritionist, call the Consumer Nutrition Hotline (see Appendix). You can get your questions answered and learn more about how to provide a healthy diet for your baby.

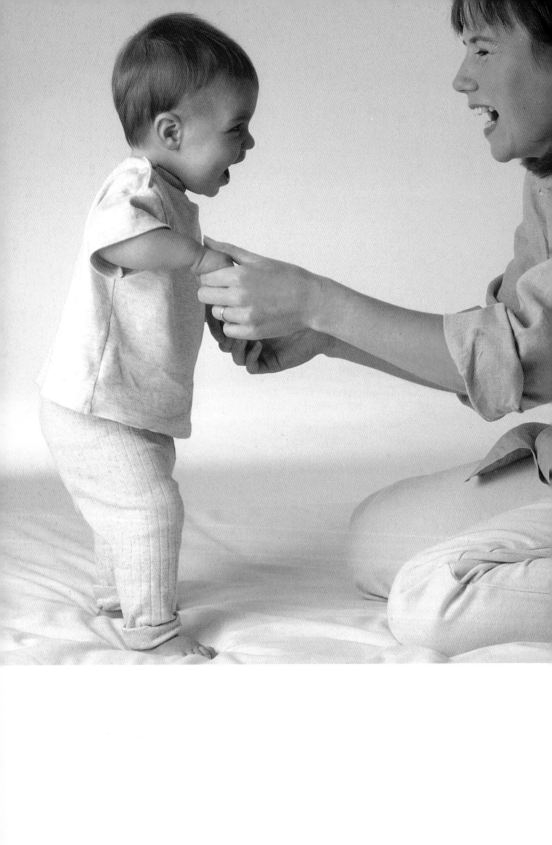

9

Growing
and
Changing

" *When Jimmy was ten months old, he
learned he could walk anywhere as long
as someone held his hand. He became
a little tyrant. He'd pull himself up on
your leg and fuss until you took him
for a walk. He was so pleased that he
refused to try walking alone for months.
As soon as you let go of his hand, plop,
he'd sit down on his bottom. Then he'd
complain loudly until someone agreed
to take him walking again.* "

FROM BABY TO TODDLER

In the first 18 months, your baby grows faster than he ever will again in his whole life. His physical skills also grow at an amazing rate. He begins as a helpless infant with very little control over his body. With a lot of practice, he becomes an upright, mobile little person. He explores the world around him with hands that push, pull, poke, squeeze and turn. One of the great joys of being a parent is to watch and encourage your baby to develop.

HOW YOUR BABY GROWS

Your baby's growth is fastest at birth. Though the rate slowly drops, he still grows quickly until about age three. Then he enters the growth lull of childhood. This lasts until the spurt at adolescence.

Some babies grow faster than others. Larger babies, who will often become larger adults, tend to gain both weight and height more quickly than smaller babies. A baby will often double his birthweight by about four to six months and triple it by one year. Length increases by about one quarter in the first year. Because your baby is a unique person, there is no way to tell exactly how fast he will grow.

Your baby may lose a few ounces right after birth. Then he will begin to gain weight, about 5 or 6 ounces (150g to 175g) per week (see page 124). Weight gain may not be steady, though. He is likely to have a series of gains and rests, with a pattern of fairly steady growth. He should look well, be alert and have plenty of energy. He should also be fairly social and show interest in the people around him.

As your baby grows, his body proportions change. His head is fairly large at birth. It grows quickly through the first year, twice as much as it will in the next 11 years. This reflects crucial brain growth. A young baby's legs are rather short. But they begin to grow longer and stronger. By the time a baby walks, he has less round tummy and more long legs.

As long as your baby is well fed, he will grow to reach his genetic potential. At times of illness, growth may slow down. But a "catch-up" period of faster growth may follow.

HOW YOUR BABY DEVELOPS

"With your first, you want her to do everything. I would hold one hand behind Emma's back and say, 'Look, she can sit up.' It's like a race to see whose baby can do things first, which is so silly. They all do things in their own way. " HELEN

A tape measure and scales can measure growth. But "What is he doing now?" will gauge the way your baby develops. New skills like holding his own hand or sitting up, crawling and walking appear one after the other. Your baby puts a lot of effort and attention into learning them. The sequence is about the same for every baby. It moves from head to foot and from the middle to the edges. So first your baby gains control of his eye and head movements. Arm control comes before leg control. He can make large movements with his whole arm from the shoulder before he can control the movements of his hand. And he can use the whole hand before he masters finger movements.

Each baby develops through stages in roughly the same order. But babies differ in how quickly they move through each stage. So all age guides are only estimates. Genetic inheritance plays a big part. It provides a blueprint for the whole process of maturing. A baby's nervous system, muscles and senses must mature to a certain point before he will be able to master certain skills. Rate of maturing tends to run in families. There may be a family of early walkers or late walkers. Neither will be better or worse at walking in the long run.

How you help your baby to develop new skills does have an impact, too. It is true that if your baby is not ready to walk, for example, you cannot teach him

A baby's head is big for his body because of the early and rapid growth of the brain. As his nervous system matures, he slowly gains control over his body. His body control moves down, from head to arms and then to legs. It also moves outward, from trunk to limbs to fingers and toes.

GROWTH CHARTS

Each time you visit a doctor or clinic, your baby will be weighed. His or her weight will be plotted on growth charts like the ones shown below. Weight and height charts are designed to detect any problems with your child's growth that might show up. The printed lines—percentiles—show the upper and lower limits within which most children fall. But such growth charts tend to reflect growth patterns of bottle-fed babies. Healthy breast-fed babies who are not fed solids before 4 to 6 months of age tend to grow a little more slowly. And fewer breast-fed babies become fat children or fat adults. Your doctor or nurse will look for a steady rate of growth to confirm your child's good health. Your baby's growth will probably follow the percentile lines on the chart.

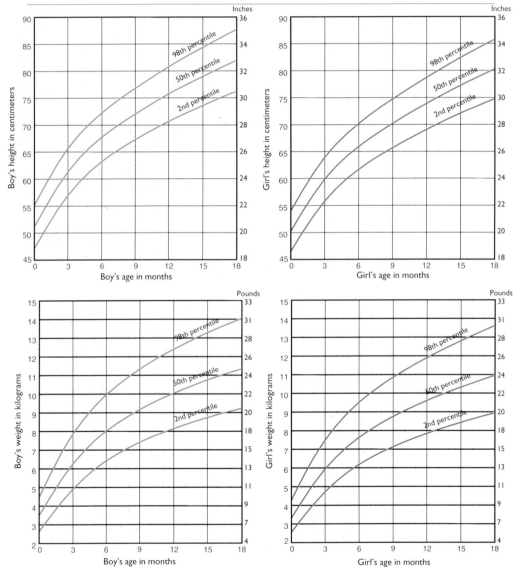

to walk. But once he is ready, give him support when he needs it. Show excitement and praise his efforts. He may walk sooner than if you leave him strapped in a stroller or swing for much of the day.

You can help your baby develop by providing a rich environment to capture his interest. You also help by getting involved. Play with him and praise what he does. He really likes to please you. But you also need to know when to let him learn things in his own way. He knows best what he needs to master in order to move on to the next challenge. Sometimes there will be a focused look on your baby's face as he watches his own movements. When you see him focus on something, don't distract him. Let him practice. He'll let you know when he's ready for something more.

Your baby likes to learn new skills. She will love to practice them on her own. She will also love it when you encourage her. Show her you share her pleasure in the new things she can do.

Head control

Birth: Your baby has little control over her heavy head. She needs you to support it in lifting and holding her.

One month: When lying on her tummy, she can turn her head from side to side and lift it. But she still needs her head and neck supported.

Two months: She can lift her head up and hold it briefly.

Three months: Her neck and upper back muscles have become stronger. When she is on her tummy, she can lift and hold her head up as she props herself on her forearms. When on her back, her head no longer falls back as you lift her.

Eyes and hands work together as she learns to measure distance with her eyes. She studies what effect her reaching or swinging arms have on objects in space. Bright colors and shapes attract her. They encourage her to reach out and explore.

Five months: When she is on her back and you pick her up, she lifts her head right up to help. She has good strength in her neck, arms and upper body. She may have enough strength to roll over.

Using hands

We must learn to connect what our eyes see to what our hands can do. This is the key to diverse human skills, whether hammering, cooking, writing or drawing. The space around your baby is new. She will soon learn to use her hands to find, feel and grasp the objects she sees. Then she will have mastered a great tool for being active in the world.

Birth: Your baby's *grasp reflex* makes her fingers close on anything touching her palm. She will need to lose the reflex before she can learn to grasp things on purpose. Most of the time her hands are closed.

TIP: Put bright simple pictures and objects about 10 inches (25cm) away for her to look at. She will learn to focus her vision on things around her. This is the first step to reaching out to explore with her hands.

Two months: Your baby follows moving objects with her eyes. She makes reaching movements with her whole arm as her hand opens and closes. She may begin to watch her hands as she moves them around.

TIP: Place a toy in your baby's hand so she can feel it and see it move as she moves her arm. A rattle lets her hear the effect of her movement.

Three to four months: She finds her hands and brings them together to study them. With jerky movements, she will reach for objects. She'll make a broad swipe with her whole arm and fist.

TIP: Tie a piece of elastic over her crib and dangle a toy from it just within her reach. Now and then add a new toy. Or fasten something new to an older toy, such as empty thread spools, spoons and keys. New shapes and textures attract her. And those that make noises reward her efforts.

Five months: As she reaches, she looks back and forth from the object to her hand to measure the distance. Now she can grasp an object. She'll use her whole hand to grab it. She often brings the other hand to hold it.

TIP: Whatever she grabs will go straight into her mouth for her to explore. Be sure there are no sharp edges. And don't leave small objects that she could choke on within her reach.

Six to seven months: Now she reaches with confidence. She knows just how far away something is. She holds objects as if she were wearing a mitten, with her thumb away from her fingers. She may play with her toes.

TIP: Hold out toys and let her take them from you. She will enjoy watching you make toys work.

Eight to nine months: Her grip is now less clumsy. She holds an object between her thumb and the side of her index finger. She can take a toy from you and may hold it out to you. But she still can't let go at will.

TIP: Provide toys that will make a sound or movement. Play games that let your baby practice pulling, banging and turning her wrist.

Ten to 12 months: She has learned to let go. She loves to drop things over and over. She may throw things. She can point. She can also pick up small objects by pinching them between thumb and index finger. She can poke objects into holes and hold a crayon. She will enjoy "pat-a-cake," clapping and may wave goodbye to people.

With a strong back, coordinated arm movements and confident grasp, a baby can decide what he wants to do and then do it. This is how he develops his own will and sense of being competent in the world around him.

TIP: Play "pick up" with her. Retrieve the object she throws or drops time and again. Then tie a toy onto her crib or chair with string so she can pull it back all by herself.

Thirteen to 15 months: She can hold two objects in the same hand. She may pull off her socks.

TIP: Let her put objects into a container one by one. Give her a saucepan and lid. Empty yogurt containers or plastic cups make great toys.

Fifteen to 18 months: She can build a tower of three blocks. She feeds herself and can scribble with pens or crayons.

TIP: Let her feed herself, even if she's messy. Play with her to show her activities she can copy.

Sitting up

Being upright is great for your baby because he can look around better. Even in the first few weeks, you can put him in an infant seat or car seat. This will give firm support for his back in a slightly inclined position. He will feel more a part of things going on around him.

As he becomes stronger, you can prop him up in the corner of a sofa with cushions for support. Or hold him in a sitting position on your lap. Give him just as much support under the arms as he needs. This gives him a chance to use the muscles that will help him to sit up.

Four months: Your baby's back is now strong enough for him to sit upright with support on the sides so he won't slip sideways. He can now enjoy the view if he sits in a baby backpack.

Six to seven months: He may sit alone for a few seconds, but can still lose his balance. To sit alone, he may need his hands on the floor for support. When propped with cushions, his hands are free for play.

Eight months: He now sits well without support. But he can't move much without falling over.

Nine months: He has become confident of his balance. He can lean over to reach something and come back to sitting. He can twist around sideways. Leave a few toys on the floor within his reach. He may use his broader range of movement to pick up and discard things as he plays.

Crawling

Some babies never crawl but go straight to pulling themselves up and walking. Or they may get around on their bottoms by scooting. Others are so pleased with the crawling that they don't seem to care about walking. Crawling styles vary, too. There is the classic forward movement, as well as backward crawls, a kind of "bear walk," and sideways crab steps.

Crawling takes strength and practice. Crawling also helps your baby's brain develop. When he is alert and awake, spread a clean blanket or quilt

A baby's basic nature can affect the skills he works on. One baby may be adept at fine-motor control and build a tower with ease while not yet walking. Another may not have time for such pursuits because he is eager to be up and around.

over a carpet on the floor. Put him in the center of it, on his tummy. His hands and feet should be bare. Put some brightly colored toys within his reach. Then sit down beside him and encourage him to reach, move and creep. The weight of his body may frustrate him. But if you offer a lot of support, the exercise will help him grow stronger.

Four months: When lying on his stomach, your baby will be able to lift himself up high with his weight on his arms. He may also lift both arms and legs and rock on his stomach, as if he can't wait to take off.

Six months: He can now raise himself into a crawling position. He may creep a bit or rock back and forth on hands and knees.

Seven months: He begins to take his weight forward onto his arms. He may pull a knee up underneath him.

TIP: Encourage him to crawl when it looks like he's ready. Offer him a toy that's just out of reach. Praise his efforts to move toward it.

Eight to nine months: He's off! Once your baby is mobile, be very careful about household safety (see page 184).

Walking—up and away

Most babies take their first solo steps, with legs wide apart and elbows high, between nine and 15 months. Walking follows a lot of practice standing and moving around with support. The normal age range is very wide, though. Some babies don't mature into walking until around 18 months.

Three months: Hold your baby in a standing position on your knees as you talk to her. She will support some of her weight with her legs.

Six months: Hold her in a standing position. She now begins to bounce up and down. She may enjoy a bouncer to exercise her leg muscles. (But don't use baby walkers. Doctors have found they can harm the way a baby develops.)

Bare feet indoors give a better grip on the floor and help keep feet healthy. Bare feet help your baby exercise the right muscles and distribute weight correctly. On cold floors, socks with grips on the bottom are the next best thing. Save shoes for walking outdoors.

Eight months: When held upright, she can step with her feet. But her knees may sag under her weight after a while.

Nine months: She can pull herself up on furniture. But for a while she can't get back down again.

Ten to 12 months: With furniture for support, she begins to walk. First she moves with her hands sliding along a surface. Then she moves from one support to another. As her skill and confidence grow, she will let go of a support and take a step to reach you. By one year, some babies will be taking a few steps on their own.

> **"** *I had an awful moment when Kendra was six months old. She got around by rolling. I'd gone out of the kitchen for just a minute. I came back and she'd rolled all the way across the floor. She had her face in the dog's bowl and was eating the food! I called the nurse and asked for advice. She said, 'The dog eats the food and he's all right, isn't he? Well, Kendra should be OK.* **"** ANNE

Fifteen months: She still walks with feet wide apart and arms out for balance. But now she can stand up without support instead of pulling herself up. Once walking, she may not be able to stop without falling down.

Eighteen months: Her arms are closer to her sides now. She has much more control. She can stop or turn as she walks. She can bend down to pick something up and stand again. And she can push or pull large toys.

TIPS: Bare feet indoors will help your baby grip the floor. Bare feet also help her foot muscles develop well. If the floor is cold, try soft socks with grips on the soles. Once your baby is walking by holding onto furniture, arrange things to make the gaps small enough to reach between. But don't use baby walkers. Doctors have learned they can interfere with a baby's normal development.

IS SOMETHING WRONG?

Most parents are eager for their baby to reach the next milestone. They may begin to feel anxious if their baby seems to lag weeks behind others in certain skills. It may be hard not to compare your baby with others. But keep in mind that babies differ widely in the rate at which they develop. Their natures differ, too. One baby can be eager and active while another prefers to babble and learn to talk.

If you are worried about your baby's development, discuss your concern with your doctor. She will probably put your mind at rest. But you can arrange for a thorough assessment if you'd like. You know your baby best. Your feeling that something may be wrong should not be ignored. It can mean that a careful checkup is needed.

Some problems show up at birth. But others may appear as the weeks and months pass and the baby does not follow the normal sequence of development. Perhaps the baby is floppy and does not develop muscle tone to control his head or sit up. Or perhaps visual problems interfere with reaching and grasping. The sooner problems like this are spotted, the sooner help can be given.

With love and care, both to physical and mental needs, a child with Down syndrome can develop into an active and positive member of a family, and of society. Parents often say that while the demands are great, they are well rewarded by the child's joy and affection.

When it is learned that a baby has a disability, there may be profound shock and grief for parents. They may feel as if they have lost their perfect child. But when a problem is discovered some time after birth, the baby is already loved and accepted as a unique person. The family can be helped to deal with the tragic news by the healthcare provider. He can provide counselling. He will also provide clear guidance in caring for the child. Contact other parents whose children have similar problems (see Appendix). They can provide help in sharing fears for the future. And they can offer useful advice and help.

The baby is already learning to cope. He is not aware of a problem. Parents should be given a prediction that is as accurate as possible of the effects of their baby's problem. But the effect on a baby depends partly on the help he receives. The extra care the baby requires can put an enormous strain on a whole family far into the future. And the rewards parents expect from their growing child may not be there. On the other hand, a different kind of giving can result in a different kind of reward. Each small advance is a triumph. Some families have found that a child with a disability draws them closer together. Responding to the challenge can bring them a richer outlook on life.

PHYSICAL MILESTONES

What baby can do	Approximate age
Roll over, front to back	4-6 months
Roll over, back to front	5-7 months
Sit without support	6-9 months
Crawl	9-11 months
Walk with support	10-12 months
Walk alone	13-18 months

TEETH

All of your baby's first teeth are in the jaws before birth. The permanent teeth have even started to form. Just when they begin to appear is governed by genes. Nothing in diet or habits will have much effect on when teething begins. Diet does have a large influence, though, on the strength and health of the teeth. Healthy teeth start with a good diet rich in calcium for the mother during pregnancy. And your baby needs plenty of calcium right through childhood.

A baby tooth is rarely present at birth. For some babies, it can be a year before teething begins. But most babies cut their first tooth around four to six months of age.

Some babies aren't bothered by teething. One day you might just find that a tooth has appeared. Or you may notice a light bulge on the gum or a red patch on the gum and cheek. A tooth may follow in a day or two. Other babies have much more discomfort with teething. They may be cranky. They may wake in the night. They may drool more than usual. Or they may cry during feeding or if a spoon hits the sore spot on the gum.

Order of teething

The order in which teeth appear is the same for almost all babies, even though the timing differs. The first teeth to appear are the central bottom pair of incisors. Most of the time they come in at four to six months. These are followed by the two central top incisors. Then come the top teeth on either side of those. Then the next bottom incisors appear. By about one year, the average baby will have all four center cutting teeth, top and bottom.

A gap then appears. The lower and upper molars, grinding teeth farther back in the mouth, arrive at around 12 to 14 months. The gap is filled in by the pointed canine teeth. They begin to appear at around 18 months. The set of baby teeth will only be complete when the second set of molars appears at the back at around age six (see page 134).

Caring for teeth

Your baby's first teeth will be replaced later in childhood by the permanent teeth. But baby teeth are still of great importance. They are needed through childhood for eating and good appearance. And they maintain the correct positions to guide the permanent teeth into place. Good habits in caring for teeth start in babyhood and can last your child a lifetime.

A good diet will help keep teeth and gums healthy by providing the right nutrients for growth. Fluoride may be added to the water supply where you live. This also helps form strong tooth enamel. Check with your dentist about fluoride in your area.

You can also prevent tooth decay by staying away from certain foods. Decay occurs when bacteria feed on a sticky coating of plaque on the teeth.

These bacteria secrete acid, which eats into the teeth. So you can protect teeth by preventing plaque from forming. Sticky sweets and sugared foods, including drinks, form the most plaque. Raw fruits and vegetables help clean the teeth. If you do give your baby sweets or puddings, serve them at meal-times. Then clean the teeth or at least rinse with water afterwards. Don't give your baby sweet foods or drinks between meals. The sugar may stay on the teeth for hours.

Your baby's teeth and gums should be cleaned daily as soon as teething begins. Wipe the gums to help remove the milky residue that can stick to teeth as they emerge. Wet a small gauze square and use it to rub your baby's teeth and gums once or twice a day. As she approaches one year, give her a baby toothbrush. Let her copy you as you brush your teeth. You will still need to clean her teeth for her until she is about three years old. But she will be learning to care for her teeth.

Easing teething pain

Most teething gels for numbing sore gums should not be used. Your baby will swallow the medicine. With all the teething he will do in the first year, that would amount to quite a lot. Cold is soothing. You could give him a fluid-filled teether cooled in the refrigerator, but not frozen. (A frozen teether could cause frostbite.) A carrot is good for him to gnaw on. Or you could rub his gum with your finger. If he is very fretful in the night, you could give him one dose of acetaminophen (Tylenol®) to help him sleep. But don't make a habit of it.

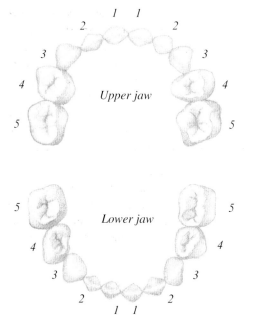

Upper jaw
1 Central incisors 6-8 months
2 Lateral incisors 8-10 months
3 Canines 18 months
4 First molars 12-14 months
5 Second molars 6 years

Lower jaw
1 Central incisors 4-6 months
2 Lateral incisors 10-12 months
3 Canines 18 months
4 First molars 12-14 months
5 Second molars 6 years

Be sure not to dismiss signs of illness as teething. Fever, vomiting, diarrhea or signs of a cold do not come from teething. See your doctor about any of these symptoms.

QUESTIONS AND ANSWERS

Q: How soon can I tell if my baby will be left-handed or right-handed?
A: Signs of a preference for one hand or the other may show up from the start. Watch which way your baby turns his head when lying down. Once he starts to reach for things, he may show a preference. He may tend to reach first with one hand. Some babies seem to have a definite one-sided dominance early on and stick to it. But most use either hand until they are about one year old. Even after that, small children may change hands for different tasks. A clear dominance of one hand over the other may not emerge for some time. A few remain ambidextrous, using either hand equally.

Q: Over a month ago, my little girl took a few steps on her own. But she seems to have forgotten all about it and now she just crawls. Is this normal?
A: New skills don't grow steadily, but in fits and starts. It is normal for a baby to have a spurt and do something new and then just practice until she has mastered it, without going on to the next step. Or she may leave it while she works on something else. Your daughter won't have forgotten how to walk. She may have just put it on a back burner while she tries out a few words. When she's ready, she may surprise you by taking off on two feet all of a sudden.

Q: Now that my baby is crawling, I use a stair gate. But she loves the stairs and always makes a beeline for them. When can she learn about stairs?
A: Babies do like to climb. So she can go up stairs soon after she can crawl. It's a good idea to teach her now, in case she ever does find stairs unguarded. Let her crawl up, with you behind her. And if you ever find her going up, don't call and distract her. That could cause a fall. Just get behind her. With you below her on the stairs, show her how to go down by crawling backwards. She will crawl up and down stairs for some time after she can walk. But between 18 months and two years, she'll begin to walk up and down stairs.

Q: Should I give my baby fluoride drops to protect her teeth?
A: Fluoride helps prevent tooth decay by making the tooth enamel harder. In some places, the water supply contains fluoride. In others, children can receive fluoride drops or chewable tablets. Check with your dentist about the water where you live. And ask her whether she recommends fluoride supplements for your baby.

10

Learning

“ *I'm stunned at how much he's learned in a few short months. He picks things up so fast. You can almost see the wheels turning as he puts two and two together. Sometimes when he doesn't want to go to sleep, it seems he's just too busy finding out about things to bother with sleep.* ”

FROM THE WORLD OF THE SENSES

Think of a dream. Something may appear one minute in it and vanish the next. A person may somehow become a tree or turn into someone else the next time you look. You may float through space or fall without ever reaching the ground. You don't know why or how things happen here. You may shake your head and wonder when you wake up. But it all seemed to make sense at the time. You weren't using the rules of logic. You just took it all as it came.

To a new baby, life may be something like this—but even more so. A baby has no knowledge of the past or thought of the future. But she receives a wealth of impressions through her senses. Light, color, sound, smell, taste and contact through touch come and go. She doesn't know what causes them. She doesn't even know that she is a separate being and that her own waving hand belongs to her.

But from the start, she is intelligent. She has much to learn. She begins, right away, to store her impressions and make sense of the world around her. Human babies develop for a longer period of time than all other animals. That's because we don't behave from instinct, most of the time. Human brainpower allows us to reason. We predict and solve problems. And we need time for all that learning.

PARENTS AS TEACHERS

In many ways, you are the most important teachers your baby will ever have. You help to set the right conditions for her intelligence to blossom. With your help, she learns how to learn. You help her to become confident enough to reach out, take a chance, explore and discover.

Feeling Secure

By loving your baby and caring for her, you help her to feel secure. She knows that she will be looked after. She learns to trust that she will be safe and her needs will be met. And she develops the confidence to try new things. As she grows, she will be eager to explore as long as you are nearby. She will run back to you whenever she needs the comfort of your presence.

Her growing trust in life and in you is essential for her to reach her full potential. This doesn't mean that she always has to be happy or that you must instantly solve all her problems. Life isn't like that. Sometimes help isn't there right away. And there are no magic solutions to some problems. Being "good enough" parents means meeting her needs most of the time. In fact, she will feel more secure when she learns that it's not the end of the world to feel unhappy or to fail at something. If she trusts the loving care behind her, she can learn to take the bumps and hurdles in stride and try again.

Stimulation

When you provide stimulating surroundings, you introduce your baby to the world. You give her things to look at and touch, play with and listen to. All day long you talk to her and help her to notice and respond to things around her. Be careful, though, not to load her up with too much stimulation. She can focus better on one thing at a time. Too much constant noise and movement will interfere with her efforts to make sense of things. Give her the chance to learn how to direct her attention for herself. Let her choose what to concentrate on from among all the choices around her.

Responding

The best education always starts where the learner is and takes him or her one step further. Nobody can help your baby learn better than you. You know her best and can respond to her signals. You are aware of what interests her and what she is trying to do. So you can repeat the action she is focused on for her. When she's had enough of that, you can vary it a little to give her a new view. Your response increases her interest, too, because she loves your involvement.

Safety

Safe surroundings are important for your baby's learning. In a safe space, she can explore without always being told "no." This lets her be more confident and curious. And you are more relaxed. (See page 165, "Safety Tips," and pages 183 to 184 on accident prevention and home safety.)

You are your baby's first teacher. When you do things with her, you build the foundation of her learning for life. Even when a child is learning in school, the time spent with parents at home is one of the biggest factors in her continued success.

Help

Be a partner in your baby's adventures. Offer a helping hand when she wants to do something she can't yet do. You will expand her world and cut down on frustration. For instance, maybe she wants to build a tower of three blocks so she can knock them down again. But it keeps falling over as she tries to put on the top block. Provide tactful help by holding the bottom blocks steady as she places the third on top. This will allow her to complete the process. Then she may want to repeat it over and over to make sure that hitting them with her hand always has the same effect.

HOW BABIES LEARN

Researchers study the way babies learn and how they come to understand the world. They watch babies' reactions to things. They can't tell what a baby is thinking, but they can make good guesses based on how he behaves. Which picture does a baby look at longest? Does his heartrate speed up when something happens?

You might enjoy watching your baby's growing understanding. Watch how he reacts at different ages. If you move a toy across his vision, does he follow it with his eyes? If it disappears from his view, does he seem surprised when it reappears? Or does he act as if he expected it? Once he can sit up, you can show him a toy and then hide it under a cloth. At what age does he lift the cloth to look for it? When does he begin to predict based on what he has learned? When does he seem to know getting the backpack means you are going out?

Taking your baby out can be great fun! It gives him the chance to learn about his world. Most babies enjoy a change of scene, fresh air and new sights and sounds. A very young baby can be taken out in a stroller or a sling. The rhythmic movement is likely to send him to sleep. By about four months, he may prefer a forward-facing stroller or baby backpack, which gives him a better view.

The senses

Babies learn about the world through their senses. They may focus most on what they can see and hear. Human faces interest babies most. But your baby will also have interest in simple patterns in strong colors. A baby stores sense impressions in his memory. Soon he begins to recognize familiar images. He shows more interest in something slightly different from the familiar, rather than something totally new.

"Once, when Matthew was only a few weeks old, I'd cut out some pictures from bright-colored pieces of felt and glued them onto his crib bumper. The first time he saw them, as I laid him in his crib at night, was like he'd had an electric jolt, he was so excited. He cried when I turned the light off. I had to leave it on for him to lie there and study the shapes and colors. " JANE

Predictions and practice

Just like a scientist, your baby begins his "study" by observing the world around him. He soon starts to sort out his impressions into patterns. He finds that certain things go together. For instance, when he hears your voice he expects you to appear. And he may connect you with contact and food.

He begins to predict things. And he wants to test whether his predictions are right. If he swings his arm and it hits the hanging rattle, will it always move and make a sound? When he sits in his highchair and lets go of a toy, will it always fall to the floor? In the bath, when he slaps down his arms, will water fly? Later, when he reaches for a stream of running water, why can't he grab and hold it? As he learns, he must test what happens over and over until he is sure he has got it right.

Imitation

Your baby also learns by copying you. At first he imitates by instinct. He copies your facial expressions without knowing he is doing it. But slowly it comes more under his control. When he copies your actions, sounds and expressions, he tries out many skills. He cannot copy something too different from what he can already do. But if you copy his sounds and gestures, he becomes more aware of them. Then he can go on to imitate new things you add. As he grows older, he will continue to mimic your actions. You may be surprised at how detailed his perceptions of you are.

Emotions

Besides copying your actions, your baby is sensitive to your feelings and copies them, too. If you meet new events with a positive outlook and confidence, your baby will feel confident, too. But if you react with fear, your baby will pick that up. He will learn to withdraw from new situations. So encourage learning. Show feelings of pleasure in new events and share them with your baby.

GROWTH IN UNDERSTANDING

Birth to four months: A baby can recognize its mother's voice and smell when just a few days old. Your baby's visual focus is short at first. But she will follow your face with her eyes if you are close enough. Within a few weeks, she will recognize your face. Bold simple patterns attract her first. As her focus expands, she will prefer to look at objects with texture and three dimensions rather than flat, smooth objects.

By three to four months, she can remember other people and events in her daily routine, such as her feedings, baths and toys. She will laugh and coo with pleasure at familiar things. And she may not be happy with changes in her routine and caregiver.

Five to six months: Your baby shows more interest in shaking and pulling and making things happen. She is also more aware of detail now. She may become attached to a certain toy. She doesn't think objects out of her view no longer exist. But her attention span is too short for her to look for them. If you partly cover a toy with a cloth, she will pull it out. But if it is totally covered, she forgets about it and doesn't search. It's a matter of "out of sight, out of mind."

Eight to ten months: Your baby is building a view of herself as a unique person. She begins to show a will of her own. She knows her own name and quite a few other words. She also recognizes objects and people when she sees them in new places. Instead of exploring most objects by feeling them in her mouth, she uses her hands and eyes to study things. She will now look under a cloth to find a hidden toy.

Twelve to 18 months: At this age, your baby loves to get a reaction from you. She will repeat again and again something that makes you laugh—or gets you upset. She wants to experiment with things, even her food at mealtimes and water in the bath. Her attention span has grown. Now she can concentrate by herself for quite a while. She understands that flat pictures in a book stand for real objects. And she can think of something she can't see and name it. She can invent solutions to problems and may use a tool to reach something, or move a box to climb up on. She copies actions not only when she sees them, but later in the day or days later. She also begins to imagine and pretend. She makes an animal sound for a toy animal, or a sound for crashing cars. She can follow simple instructions.

WHO AM I?

One of the key things your baby learns is that he or she is a unique person who acts in the world and affects other people and things. This is the start of the self-concept, which will develop and alter throughout life. Your baby's self-concept is built upon self-knowledge, and by comparing himself with others and what they say. A healthy self-concept helps him choose worth-

while goals. But there is danger in a self-concept being too limiting to let a person reach his full potential. You don't want your child to turn away from positive experiences because "it's not me."

Even in the first year, your baby is forming his self-concept in a way that may set a pattern for life. Some of his thoughts of what he is like as a person come from you. He picks up on your reactions to him, what you encourage in him and what you say about him. Babies do have their own natures right

Your baby's self-esteem— feeling good about and liking the person he is— grows from the love he receives. Because you love him, he knows he is lovable. Whatever else he learns about himself, deep down he feels secure and happy.

from the start. But be careful not to try to pin down your baby's character and put a label on it.

If parents see their baby as "boisterous and adventurous," they may provide lots of active things to do. But they may neglect seeing his quiet, thoughtful side. He also needs a chance to develop that. Or perhaps they think he's "shy and timid." It may be that he needs to observe new things for a while before he's ready to start exploring. But with patient support, he may enjoy venturing forth and become more bold. When you have more than one child, there is a tendency to compare them and note their differences. But be careful not to push them into boxes to describe them. Labels are limits, and children often grow to fit them. What a baby needs instead is respect for his own temperament. And he needs to be encouraged to develop his potential in every sphere.

Girl or boy?

Gone are the days of rigid views of what sort of toys, activities and role in life were best for each sex. But subtle assumptions can color a baby's self-concept and learning. It is true that there are a few differences between the behavior and skills of girls and boys. For instance, girls tend to learn to talk sooner and do better at early reading. It could be, though, that boys and girls are treated in different ways from babyhood. Studies have shown that people tend to talk more and make more eye contact with baby girls. So it makes sense that they are faster at language skills. On the other hand, people tend to give baby boys more active toys and praise physical skills.

People differ more from one to another than males differ from females. So don't limit your baby by supporting either a boyish or girlish side. Follow his or her lead in interests and activities. And develop all your baby's qualities.

A MIND OF HIS OWN

At first, your baby just accepts things as they come. Soon he learns to control his actions. And he finds that his actions can have an effect. Now he has his own thoughts and develops a will to back them up.

When your baby begins to assert his own will, he adds a new dimension to your lives. Things begin to be more two-way rather than all the thoughts and decisions coming from you. There are sure to be times of conflict when you don't accept what he wants to do.

Conflict

Why might you object to your baby's behavior? A very valid reason is danger. Babyproof your home to minimize the number of times you must stop your baby from exploring for safety concerns. Even so, there is always something your baby can climb on or into or grab that poses a danger. On the other hand, you don't want to be too protective and stop your baby from challenges. This can prevent him from mastering new skills. Sometimes you can let him try what he wants to do, while you stand by. You will need to use your judgment and knowledge of your baby's skills to decide how much you can allow.

You might want to stop some behavior because it makes too much mess and work for you. Maybe he wants to learn about petroleum jelly by dipping his hand in the jar. Or he wants to pull all the pans and lids to the kitchen floor for the sixth time that day. But you don't want to pick it up again.

" I feel like a policeman all day long— 'Don't touch this, don't touch that.' We've moved the breakable things. But he goes after the stereo, the plants and opens doors. I can say 'no.' But I don't think he remembers from one minute to the next what I don't want him to do. He doesn't play with things I put out for him. For peace, I take him for long walks in the stroller and he loves that. " SALLY

144

TEACHING YOUR BABY

- *If you hang up a mobile toy for your baby, alter just one thing at a time for greatest interest.*
- *Let your baby learn about all sorts of things, not just smooth, bright, plastic toys. Give objects made of wood, metal, cloth of different textures and crinkly paper.*
- *It's easy to overload a young baby's senses. Don't permit a hectic atmosphere with constant background noise.*
- *Put different substances, such as perfume, vinegar, lemon juice and vanilla on balls of cotton. Hold them for your baby to smell.*
- *Play peek-a-boo with your baby. It's fun! It also shows that you haven't really disappeared just because you are covered up.*
- *Start math concepts by talking about things being empty, full, big, little, "one" and "two" objects.*
- *See if your baby can begin to sort objects. Put clothes pins in one pan and spoons in another, or sort by color.*
- *Take time doing daily routines and talk about them. This provides fertile ground for learning.*
- *Rely on your baby's curious nature for learning. Don't try to program topics. And above all, let it all be fun!*

Sometimes you might be in too much of a hurry to let him do things in his own way. When you are in a rush to get home and make dinner, you may not be able to let him toddle behind the market basket "helping" you push it. Instead, you want to put him in the seat so you can move around more quickly.

Distracting

When you must stop your baby's behavior, the best tactic is to direct his attention to something else. If he has grabbed something dangerous, take it away with one hand. But offer something else with the other. Talk to him about what you are offering as a distraction. He will accept it most of the time. Spot signs of trouble coming and use distraction quickly, before he gets too set on what he wants to do. In this way, you can steer clear of most head-on conflicts.

Saying "no"

Sometimes a quick response is needed. You might have to move fast to get him out of danger. And other times distraction may not work. At these times, you will have to say "no" to your baby, take something away or move him. By about eight months, your baby can understand what "no" means. And if you save it for times when you really need it, "no" can have a strong impact.

There is no need to say "no" with a shout. And a baby should never be spanked, which will frighten and confuse him. Your firm tone of voice, the look on your face and your manner will convince him.

Your baby wants your attention and your approval. If he tries to get a reaction by doing something you have said "no" to, don't reward him with your attention by making a big fuss. Remove the source of the trouble. Or remove him from the scene if you must, with little comment. Then give him plenty of hugs and smiles when he is doing something you approve of.

Never naughty

When a baby pulls the cat's tail, knocks over your best lamp or spills his milk on the floor, he is not being naughty. He just doesn't understand about someone else feeling pain or caring about a lamp or a mess on the floor. So stop him in what he's doing, if you must. And let him know that you dislike his behavior. Tell him it hurts, or it's a nuisance. But don't say he is "bad" for doing it. He needs to know that you still love him and approve of him, even when you don't like what he does. And he needs you to teach him what you expect of him.

When you need to stop your baby from doing something, remember that she doesn't know any better. Teach her with patience and respect. Let her know why her behavior isn't all right. You will help her learn to temper what she wants with the needs and feelings of others.

QUESTIONS AND ANSWERS

Q: Can my baby learn by watching television?

A: Television has little to offer a baby. It may surround the baby with the rhythm and sounds of language, but she can't pick out separate words. It is no substitute for real interactions. The richest dialog with a baby is based on what she can really see and feel. Because television offers so little, most babies don't show much interest in it. Having it on much of the time can teach them to tune things out rather than be alert and interested.

Q: At 12 months, my baby always plays with his food and it ends up all over. Should I stop him and try to start teaching him table manners?

A: A 1-year-old does learn by exploring his food. He will feel it and see what it will do as well as eat it. At some point, though, he crosses the line between learning as part of eating and simple playing. And you don't need another mess to clean up. Table manners are really about respecting how others feel. So if you feel he is not really studying his food, but just enjoys smearing or throwing it, put a stop to it. Just move him away from the table with little comment. He'll soon learn where you draw the line.

Q: When I take my baby daughter to a mother-baby group, the other babies crawl around but she is timid and clingy. Will she be behind the others because she doesn't get out and do things?

A: Being bold and exploring new places is a good way for babies to learn. But it can only happen when a baby is ready. If you try to force independence too soon, you can prolong the clinginess. It can frighten a baby and make her feel less confident. Sit down on the floor with your baby. Let her explore things from a feeling of safety near you. Don't worry about her learning. It happens in spurts. She can discover a lot in a short time when she's ready.

Q: At what age do babies learn to play together? Do they need contact with other babies to learn to be sociable?

A: Most babies seem to enjoy having other children around. By the time they are a few months old, they are aware of other babies. At a year or so, they may enjoy playing near another baby. They may even copy each other. But they won't really play together for another year. In the meantime, your baby learns to be sociable from being with you.

Q: My baby is becoming headstrong about little things like not sitting in his chair when his meal is ready. Should I insist so he learns to behave?

A: Good discipline lies in respecting other people's feelings. One way to teach that to your baby is to show respect for him. When he's playing and it's time for a meal, don't whisk him away. Tell him and get his cooperation. Let him make choices, such as to wear his boots around the house. Let him feel important by helping you put the carrots in the pan for dinner. He copies you in most things—including attitude. If you show him courtesy, he will learn to show you courtesy, too.

11

First Words

"She didn't say a single word until she was nearly two years old. Sometimes I wondered if she was ever going to speak at all. But just listen to her talking now! Even before she spoke, she always managed to make herself understood."

NATURAL ABILITY

You look forward to a long cozy chat, a whispered secret, a joke or a story. No wonder the prospect of your baby beginning to speak holds such promise. Your lives are enriched. And you can learn just what your baby thinks once he begins to speak. Using language well will also help him learn throughout life.

Learning to talk does come naturally. At times, it seems that a baby soaks language up like a sponge, without effort. In contrast, adults must work hard to learn a foreign language. But though babies are born with the ability to learn to speak, language skills don't come by themselves. They must be learned. Throughout the first year of life, your baby is learning the basic skills that prepare him for his first words.

Telling you something in words is a long way from his first days. Crying was his only way to express a need then. A newborn baby's vocal cords are like a hollow tube. His throat and tongue must mature before he can learn to make and control a range of sounds. He must also be able to hear the sounds he makes and compare them with other sounds around him. He has to learn that a certain sound stands for a certain thing or concept. He has to learn that words have meaning. And he must want to tell you something. You have a key part to play in helping your baby prepare for speaking.

ON TO TALKING

In the first month, your baby develops his lips, tongue and vocal cords as he nurses, sucks his fist and makes small noises. He listens to human speech with more interest than any other sound. In fact, he begins to pick up the rhythm of language. You may observe him making tiny movements with his whole body in time with speech. He will also watch you, and your mouth, as you speak to him.

At six weeks, your baby responds to a voice by smiling. When he looks at you, he may open and close his mouth as though he were trying to talk. He may also have begun to have "talks." He takes turns with you as he gurgles, waits for your reply and then gurgles again.

By three months, your baby likes to make cooing sounds, "aah" or "oo." He loves to entertain himself with the sounds. When he has someone's attention, he'll coo even more. He notices when you make eye contact with him. He will start "talks" now. And he'll watch your mouth closely when you respond to him.

❝A lot of people say their baby's first word is 'Dada,' or maybe 'Mama.' But Stephen's was 'backpack.' He loved going for a walk in the baby backpack. When he'd see us take it down from the rack, he'd reach for it and say "backpack, backpack" until he was in it and on his way. ❞
LAURIE

It's fun to play with sounds. A baby may lie in her crib babbling happily to herself. But making sounds and responding to them is also part of being sociable. Your baby will be alert to the sounds you make. And she'll enjoy having chatty, babbling "talks" with you.

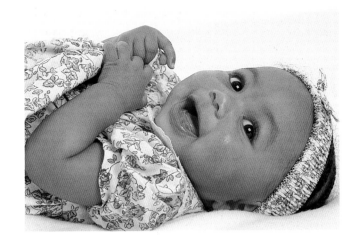

At five to six months, your baby's vocal muscles are more like an adult's. He has more control over his lips. Now he can make consonant sounds. He babbles syllables such as "da," "ma," "pa." He may spend less time making sounds than at three months. But the sound is starting to be like his native language. He learns how to make the sounds spoken around him. And he uses the rhythms and ups and downs in his voice. He will enjoy chatting with you. And he'll listen and try to copy a sound you repeat for him.

At eight months, your baby is very aware of adult speech. He will watch each person who is speaking. He may shout. And sometimes his babbling may be quite musical.

At nine to ten months, his babbling is strung together to sound just like sentences. He will enjoy your response in real sentences of similar length. He babbles alone, or with you. He understands quite a few words. And he'll be able to respond with the right actions when you tell him or ask him something. He may point when you ask "Where's Mommy's nose?"

Between ten and 12 months, your baby may say his first word. The first word grows from his use of sounds and gestures with you. Sometimes it may seem like an accident that he makes a sound you recognize as a word. Your thrilled response urges him to keep trying. Though he may not have the sounds just right, he does want you to understand what he means. And he will be delighted when you do.

From 12 to 15 months, he slowly learns new words. He may learn one or two a week. He may seem to forget about talking while he is busy learning to walk. Most of his words are the names of things. And he may love to copy animal sounds. He might include some action words such as "look" or "go." He might use describing words such as "pretty" or "hot," or social words such as "bye-bye." When he says two words, it is because he always hears them together. He thinks of them as one word, such as "all gone."

ENCOURAGE BABBLING

- *Give your baby your complete attention and return his smiles.*
- *Talk to your baby in short sentences. Then wait for a reply.*
- *Copy the sounds your baby makes.*
- *Change the sound a little—("la" instead of "da") and see if your baby can copy you.*
- *Limit background noise so your baby learns to listen more carefully.*
- *Sing and hum to your baby. Tell her nursery rhymes.*
- *Read out loud to your baby every day. Read things of interest to you, not just baby books.*
- *Talk about your daily routines. Your baby will enjoy the rhythm of your voice.*

At 18 months, naming things is a great pleasure. Your baby may begin to ask "What's that?" about things he sees. He might have a spurt and learn a few words in a short time. Or he may progress more slowly. You may hear his first two-word sentences, such as "Mommy book." You'll need to work out what he means. Is it "It's Mommy's book," or "Give Mommy the book," or "Mommy, please read the book"? He may make up his own words for things. He'll be pleased when you understand what he means. He also may make one word do general duty. For instance, he might say "cat" to mean any animal.

HOW YOU HELP

Your baby needs to listen to language to begin to learn. You provide most of the words for her eager ears. She can't pick out words when people speak around her. But she will focus intently when you speak to her one-on-one and make eye contact with her.

> " *Sometimes I have to listen closely to what I think my baby means. It doesn't come out clearly, but it is a word.*
>
> *Some of my friends don't want to use 'babytalk.' They speak to their baby as they would to an adult, using long words and sentences. They don't pay any attention when their baby makes a sound because it isn't a 'real' word yet. Their baby isn't talking yet. I wonder if it's because they don't encourage him enough.* " ANNE

Talk to your baby

Don't feel silly talking to your baby while you change her, bathe her or carry her around the house. Even if she can't understand a word you are saying, she will show her pleasure as she hears your voice. She'll let you know she likes to have you chat with her.

152

Talk to your baby as you go about daily routines. Describe and name what you are doing. She will soon learn that certain sounds always go with certain things. She will learn words such as "bath," "cup" and "bed." Help her build up her store of familiar words in this way. Then when she does start to speak for herself she will have a large store of words to put to use.

This doesn't mean that you have to chat away all the time to your baby. That could become forced and awkward for you. There are times where both you and your baby will enjoy a cozy silence. But your baby's a bright listener who will enjoy and respond to your comments on your life together.

Baby talk?

Your baby needs to hear language spoken correctly in order to learn herself. You won't be doing her any favors if you use silly names for things. But most parents have a different way of speaking to their baby than they would to an adult, which does help a baby learn.

A baby hears a slightly high-pitched voice best. You might find it natural to speak in a higher voice to your baby. You may use broad facial expressions.

Sing to your baby. It helps him listen to sounds more carefully. Strong rhythm and rhymes attract him. When he is only a few months old, he may have favorites. He might listen intently, join in with the sounds or jiggle in time.

" Sarah has just started putting two words together. I really enjoy some of the things she comes up with. Often, when we're out walking, she gets tired or is just too slow to suit me so I ask, 'Shall I carry you?' She thinks 'carry-you' is a word. So now, when she wants to be picked up, she holds up her arms and says, 'Carry-you me.' " CAROL

You may increase the inflections of your voice to make what you are saying seem exciting. You will probably use short, simple sentences. And you'll speak fairly slowly and distinctly. It will help to repeat words, such as names of things, as your baby looks at them or touches them.

As your baby learns, you are likely to stay one step ahead of her. Slowly use longer sentences. Add more descriptive words. And speak in a lower voice. This stretches her listening skills. In time, she will be able to understand conversation.

Be responsive

Have you ever tried to talk to someone who wasn't paying any attention? Chances are you became frustrated and soon gave up. The same is true for your baby. She has no reason to learn to speak if nobody listens. But she'll be encouraged when you show an interest.

Being responsive to your baby includes listening to her. Show that you are interested. When you take turns in a cooing or babbling "conversation," she feels she has an important part to play. Her gurgling noises are often triggered by having your attention when you look at her. Listen to her, then copy the sound and wait for her reply. She will recognize her own sound coming from you. And she may do it again.

ENCOURAGE TALKING

◆ *Read books with simple pictures to your baby. Repeat the names of objects. Emphasize something about the object: "This is a ball. Throw the ball!" or "It's a red ball."*

◆ *Take your baby on a walk around the house. Find things of interest to your baby. Talk about what your baby is looking at.*

◆ *Ask your baby simple questions, even before she can talk. She may be able to point or nod to answer. Then you can put it into words for her. Praise your baby's efforts. And let her know you think she is smart. Try hard to understand when your baby tries to tell you something.*

◆ *Encourage your baby to speak to other people. But interpret for him. They may not understand as well as you do.*

◆ *If someone else cares for your baby, explain what his words or signals are so he can be understood.*

Imitation is a great teacher. You are the model as your baby's language develops. She will copy your words, and your accent and way of speaking. She'll also enjoy it if you copy her sometimes.

When your baby first starts to speak, you may not understand her words. She will tend to shorten a word and leave off consonants. For "cat" she says "ca." She may also use the wrong name for things. Or she may make up her own words. At this stage, you must respond to her efforts to speak, even though they aren't perfect. Without your response, she won't feel like trying. So show her you're thrilled about her words. Respond in a way that shows you understand her. She will master the finer points later. But for now, she needs to know she has made herself understood with sounds. And that you are pleased with her. If you want to correct her mistakes and help her learn the proper way to pronounce words, be very tactful about it. She will feel put down if you make a point of it. Just repeat her words in a friendly way. Include the correction. She will notice and learn to correct herself.

Expanding baby's skills

Learning works best when it starts with what the learner already knows and moves forward one step at a time. Begin with what your baby is already doing. Then add one more step. If your baby is babbling "ta, ta, ta," you couldn't teach her to say "rabbit." But you could copy her "ta" and then change it to "ha, ha," and then "sa, sa." And she is likely to follow you.

You can also expand on your baby's language when she begins to speak. Repeat what she says in an expanded version. If she says "Dada," you can reply, "Yes, there is Daddy's car." When she says "Book," you might say, "Shall we read the book?" or "It's a nice red book." When she hears her own statement in an expanded version, she begins to see how to put words together.

Have fun with language

If your baby enjoys language, she will want to share the pleasure with you. Play taking-turn games with sounds. Laugh and praise what your baby does. Read nursery rhymes with a rhythm and rhyming pattern that babies enjoy. By about six months, your baby will enjoy songs with actions and funny, surprise endings. Your baby will love to hear you sing. Even before she can talk, she may join in with some of the sounds in a familiar song.

Language for life

Language is part of almost everything we do. You can help your baby be alert to language so he can learn to use it well. This can have a lifelong impact.

Children who enjoy words find it easiest to learn to read and do well at school. Such children have a good ear for sounds and are able to express themselves. Children who know nursery rhymes often learn to read easily. Perhaps they recognize words that sound alike and notice how they are different. All this starts right back in the first year of life, with your first babbled "talks" with your baby. Girls tend to learn to read faster than boys. They often do better in school in subjects based on language. Could this be linked to the fact that people tend to make more eye contact with girl babies and talk to them more? With boy babies, parents are more likely to provide active toys instead of conversation.

Babies differ. Some will grow into people who are good with their hands. Some will be athletes. And some will be good at speaking with others. Whatever direction your baby chooses, it will be enriched by learning to speak well with you.

Puppets are a fun way to speak with your baby. Try talking in a different voice as you move the puppet's mouth. Even though he sees your hand go into the puppet, he will think it's the puppet who is talking to him.

QUESTIONS AND ANSWERS

Q: My native language is not English. I would like my baby to learn to speak both languages. Will this just confuse him?

A: It's easy for babies to be bilingual. Your son will learn both languages now much more quickly and easily than if he learned one later in life. It is easier for the baby to sort out different languages if they are spoken to him by separate people. So you could speak to him only in your native language. And his father could speak only English to him. It may take him a little longer to speak than if he had just one language to learn. And he may mix them up a bit at first. But soon he will sort them out and be at ease with both.

Q: My first child said her first words at 11 months. But my second baby is now 15 months old and hasn't started talking. Is something wrong?

A: It's common for a baby not to speak until well into the second year. But you might also ask your doctor to check your baby. An ear infection can leave fluid in the middle ear. That could affect her hearing. Most likely there are other reasons. First children are more likely to speak early and well. They tend to get more one-on-one adult contact. Later children have much more going on around them. This can distract them from language. Older children can also interpret things for them so there is no need to speak for themselves. Try to be sure your baby gets your complete attention at a calm time every day.

Q: My baby says a few words, but none of them are very clear. Should we correct her and try to get her to say them properly?

A: If you correct your baby when she speaks, it might make her think that speaking is hard work and you aren't happy with her. It's not worth the risk of spoiling her pleasure in words to correct her. You can gently guide her by including the words in your reply. She will hear the difference and slowly become more accurate herself. You can also play sound games with her to help her hear and say sounds better. See if she will copy nonsense words like "fee, tee, hee, bee." Or try harder final consonants like "mop, mot, mom, mos."

Q: How soon can you tell if a baby is not hearing well?

A: You can't always tell if a baby has hearing problems. He may hear some types of sound but not others. And he may respond when you speak to him because he watches your lips move without hearing the sounds clearly. A deaf baby will begin to make sounds like any other baby. But by five or six months, the babbling won't change to begin to sound like speech. And the sounds will be monotonous. He will also babble less because he can't enjoy hearing the sounds he makes. If you are concerned that your baby may not be reacting to sound, see your doctor. She can arrange for special hearing tests. Babies can be fitted with hearing aids when only a few months old. And the sooner hearing loss is detected, the sooner the baby can learn to talk.

12

Play

"At first, he seemed to like his bath just to feel the warm water around him. But now he's learned that if he flails his arms, the water makes a noise and goes everywhere. He gets so excited and laughs out loud. I have to be prepared to get soaking wet. But we both enjoy it."

WHY PLAY?

A kitten will leap upon a string snaking across the floor. Puppies roll and tumble in a heap of playful yaps. Colts kick up their heels and dash across the field. And your baby laughs and gurgles with pleasure as her flailing arms set the toys dancing on her crib mobile. This is play, a crucial part of being young. It brings delight, along with a far more serious purpose.

Play is fun. Your baby is drawn to play because she enjoys it. We adults divide our time into serious work that must be done and play when our work is finished. We may think of play as "just for fun"—an optional extra. But for your baby playing is far more important than that.

Your baby's job is to become an effective and competent person. She needs to learn about her world and about how things work. She needs to interact with things around her. She needs to make her body do what she wants it to do. And she needs to learn to live with other people. In each case, play is her key.

Through play a baby observes how objects behave. She learns to control her body enough to move objects or make them do something. Then she can study them in even more detail. She is drawn by a powerful drive to explore and handle toys and household objects. And she has fun doing it. She enjoys it because it satisfies her need to learn and feel effective. So play has built-in enjoyment. But its purpose is serious. Playing is your baby's job.

Directed play?

Babies learn through play. Many toy makers design their products to help children learn. But parents may feel unsure about how to provide the right toys for their baby. Most parents have bought an expensive and well-designed toy, only to find that their baby prefers the box or wrapper it came in. The toy lies ignored on one side!

It helps to know which types of activities babies need. But there is no need to direct play in certain ways. And you don't have to try to make your baby play with the most elaborate toy instead of an old set of measuring spoons. She has an appetite to learn. She will take advantage of the world around her. She knows, better than anyone else, just what kind of play she needs right now in order to develop her skills. She knows because it pleases and satisfies her.

"At three months, Michele is too young for a rattle. She doesn't seem to get the concept yet. She just lies there taking everything in. She notices anything that moves. She spends a lot of time watching her own hands. She opens and closes them. I think that is her playing. She also loves it when she hits her mobile. It makes a noise and she gurgles back at it." LIN

You don't always need toys for your baby if you are with her. Some of her favorite games are likely to be old standbys, such as peek-a-boo and pat-a-cake. She doesn't find it boring to repeat them. And you will never again have such an attentive audience.

Babies do not all make the same choices in play. They have different characters, body types and interests. Some babies are robust and want vigorous physical play. They enjoy being bounced and tossed in the air. And they are quick to grab, push and throw. Others take quite a while to warm up to physical games. But they may love the social pleasure of pat-a-cake. Whatever your baby prefers, you can help by providing many types of play. Then let her choose what she wants to do most at the moment.

YOU ARE THE BEST TOY

A toy is something to play with. A good toy is one that can be used in a number of ways. It inspires new thoughts of play. Thus, you are the best toy of all. Right from the start, nothing attracts your baby as much as your face and your voice. As she grows, there is no end to the number of ways she can play with you.

At first, as with any toy, she observes you. She notices the feel of your skin, the rhythm of your heartbeat as you hold her close and your scent. Before long, she learns she can have an effect on you. When she cries, you will come. And when she smiles, you smile back.

Through playing with you, your baby learns how to get along with other people. She enjoys copycat games, peek-a-boo and pat-a-cake. She learns social skills. There will be times when something interests her, not for its own sake, but because you are sharing it with her.

FUN WITH OBJECTS AROUND THE HOUSE

Many things interest your baby. She'll play with all sorts of things you have around the house. Kitchen things make great toys. For instance:

- *yogurt containers*
- *whisk*
- *spatula*
- *pots and pans with lids*
- *plastic biscuit cutters*
- *cassette-tape boxes*
- *funnel*
- *measuring tape*
- *thread spools, single or several tied on a string*
- *ice-cube tray*

- *spoons, wooden and metal*
- *set of plastic measuring spoons*
- *egg carton*
- *colander*
- *key-ring*
- *cardboard box*
- *small plastic bottles*
- *pieces of fabric*
- *toilet-paper-roll tube*
- *ball of string*

You also bring new things to her. When she is a few weeks old, you move a rattle across her vision for her eyes to track. Perhaps you shake it gently so she connects what she sees with where the sounds come from. Later you show her objects she has never seen before. You play with her until she can play with them on her own. Watch for signs of boredom. Show her a new aspect to revive her interest in a familiar toy. Or show her some new things she can explore.

Your baby doesn't need you to play with her all the time, though. There are other things you need to do. And you want some time to yourself. Your baby can play by herself. But she still enjoys your company. She will feel most secure when she can see and hear you nearby. You might enjoy getting together with another parent and baby. Or join a mother-baby group. You can be near and play with your baby now and then. And at the same time, you can enjoy some adult company.

PLAYING AND GROWING

Birth to three months: Your baby likes to watch things that move. So let him watch you and other family members as they go about their daily routines. Place him where he can see the laundry flapping on the line or tree branches swaying.

He doesn't really need toys at this stage. But he might like a very light-weight rattle. He will grasp it and he may be able to put to his mouth. But he may also hit himself on the head with it. He will enjoy brightly colored patterns on a crib bumper. And he might enjoy soft toys or pictures in books that you can prop up for him to look at.

To make a crib mobile, tie some elastic across the crib and securely hang objects from it. You could tie on a rattle, large bright beads, a bunch of keys, a thread spool, a fluffy ball or shiny foil muffin cups. Three or four objects are enough at a time. Replace an object with something new every few days. Or tie something new to one of the items.

TOYS: *Rattle, mobiles, music box, soft toy.*

Four to six months: Now your baby can reach and grasp objects. He will like to feel different shapes and textures and make things happen. He'll enjoy toys that squeak, ring or rattle when moved. He likes faces and expressions. He will enjoy playing with his reflection in a mirror when you hold him up to look. He can now grasp objects within reach above him. And he'll put them in his mouth. So make sure that anything you fasten on his crib mobile is safe. When he finds his feet, at about five months, you can hang toys within reach of his feet for him to kick.

TOYS: *Rattles, teething rings, squeezy-squeaky toys, soft balls, soft doll, large bright wooden beads on a string.*

Play gives a chance to imagine and to explore. A baby "brumming" a car on the floor can imagine it is real. He has the powerful feeling of "driving." A big cardboard box can be something special—a small house with doors.

Six to ten months: Your baby is learning to control his hands and fingers. He likes to explore objects of all types and make a noise with them. Once he can sit up, he can play with more things. He will enjoy pop-up toys that bounce when he pushes them or a music box with a string he can pull. You can give him a box full of cloth squares of different colors and textures.

TOYS: *Activity center, balls, unbreakable baby mirror, nesting toys, large ball.*

Ten to 12 months: Hand movements are more organized. Your baby will like to turn, stack and explore the shapes of objects and put things inside containers. He will also enjoy being involved in household jobs. He will "help" you put things away. He'll put the washing in the machine, groceries in your basket or vegetables in the pot. Now that he's mobile, he will enjoy toys he can push or pull. Give him toys on a string he can drag along the floor. He can hold chalk, crayons or pens. But he'll have the most luck making a mark with felt-tip pens. Be sure they contain washable ink. And don't leave him alone with them. Water play becomes more involved now that he can sit in the bath.

TOYS: *Small blocks, stacking toys, wagon, kitchen utensils, toy xylophone, water toys and plastic cups for the bath, bag or small basket to put things in.*

Twelve to 18 months: Your baby is becoming much better at using his body. He will want to practice doing things that develop his muscles, his judgment of distance and balance. He may like to step on and off a low box, or walk with your slippers on. A small push-along bike will give him practice at physical skills. He also enjoys quiet play, which develops his fine-muscle control.

Babies take an interest in other babies. They often like to play beside each other. They may watch each other and copy what they see another baby doing. But it may be some time before they learn to get along well enough to play together.

◆ *When you buy toys or play equipment, check for a warning label.*
◆ *With used toys, check there are no loose parts or broken edges.*
◆ *Never give your baby something with hard, sharp edges.*
◆ *Don't give your baby small objects or toys with small parts that could come off and be swallowed.*
◆ *With soft toys, check for safety of eyes and noses. They should be sewn on, or fixed with safety backings so they won't come off.*
◆ *Be careful with items that could come apart when chewed, such as cardboard toilet paper rolls or magazine pages. Take them away once they are softened.*
◆ *Don't leave your baby alone when playing, except in a crib or playpen with safe toys, such as a rattle or board book.*

He wants you nearby for company. And he needs you to supervise for safety. But he may play for quite a while on his own. He explores in his play. He wants to learn how things work. He is learning to pretend and may enjoy toy cars, animals and dolls. He can begin to play with sand. You can buy clean sand and put it in a plastic basin on a spread of newspapers. But watch closely and teach him not to put it in his mouth. Thick paintbrushes and bold poster paint on large paper give him pleasure. He likes to watch the record it makes of his arm and hand movements.

TOYS: *Hammer toys, toy telephone, doll, animals, cars, bike, harmonica, paints, a jigsaw puzzle with simple, chunky pieces, books, water toys with holes.*

BOOKS

As soon as you can hold your baby on your lap and show her a book, you can share with her the pleasure of books and reading. When she is quite young, perhaps two or three months old, she will enjoy looking at books. She will like the colors and patterns on the pages. She'll enjoy the sound of the turning pages and the comfort of being held closely and hearing your voice. Show her any books or magazines that have pictures.

By about six months, you might read together from a book of nursery rhymes. She will enjoy the rhythmic sounds and the pictures. But she still won't recognize anything more than colors and patterns.

By the end of the first year, your baby will recognize simple pictures in books. Colorful photos or lifelike drawings of familiar objects make more sense to your baby than cartoon-type drawings. Talk about the pictures with her. And point as you name things. Ask her questions. She may begin to point in reply, or make sound effects.

Books offer the chance to be involved with things beyond your daily life. Your baby may learn to recognize and enjoy making sounds for farm or jungle animals, a steam train, a fire engine. She will also enjoy household subjects, such as mealtimes or a baby going to bed.

She will enjoy hearing you read real stories sooner than you might expect. She may not understand much of it, but her understanding will grow. From about 12 months on, your baby may enjoy stories with familiar elements, such as parents and babies, bathtime, bedtime, shopping and playing—whether the characters are people or animals. She loves repetition. Though you may get tired of saying the same words and singing the same songs day after day, she won't be bored.

Learning to love books is the start of a lifetime of pleasure. Teaching your baby to respect books can be one of her first lessons. A tattered, scribbled-on book with a dog-eared cover or no cover at all, thrown into a box of toys, does not command respect. But books that are kept in good order and belong in a certain place will become valued objects. Then the pleasures they have to offer will be more open to your baby.

Babies love to crinkle paper. If left alone with a book they will soon wad up the pages and probably tear some. This can give the wrong message about respect for books. And you will not be likely to buy many books if that is their fate.

" *Gregory loved books, as soon as he could sit up. It teaches him words, as we point to things. Because he sees us read, he sits around reading in his way. It's nice when you see him doing something you like to do. He has his own bookshelf in the kitchen where we spend a lot of time. And sometimes I take some away or put out new ones.* **"** SUE

Instead, young babies can be given cloth books. Cloth books provide bright pictures and a chance to turn pages. By about nine or ten months, books with board pages can be handled by a baby alone. Books with paper pages should be reserved for reading with you until your baby is more than a year old.

OUT AND ABOUT

Once your baby can crawl or walk, he won't like to be confined in a stroller or play-pen for long. Try to plan outings for off-peak times when there are fewer crowds and less noise. Then you can take your time and involve your baby in what you are doing. Talk about the items on the market shelves. Dawdle to look at the water running down the edge of the street. Or discuss the blossoms opening on a bush on the way home.

For car trips, your baby must always remain in an approved infant seat. A young baby is likely to be lulled to sleep by the movement and sound of the car. As your baby gets older, you may find it useful to keep a few toys in the car. Plan to include frequent breaks on long trips. Or travel at night so he is more likely to sleep.

Warm weather gives the chance to play outside. Even a young baby will enjoy lying or sitting on a blanket in the garden. Once he is mobile, there is plenty to explore outside. But you will have to keep a careful watch to make sure he doesn't pick up small stones or anything else to put in his mouth. Don't let him play on lawns that dogs might have fouled. Dog feces present a health risk to children.

Toddlers love the freedom and adventure of playing outdoors. But yards can have many hidden dangers for young explorers. Make sure your child is always carefully watched. Never leave her alone near water.

PLAYFUL EXERCISE

Physical movement is a fun way for your baby to play. When you exercise with your baby, you can help her body develop. You may enjoy exercise more in the context of a game rather than just as a way to stay fit. And the main purpose with your baby should be for her to enjoy it, too.

Birth to three months: Your baby should have a chance to exercise every day. Give her some time for free movement on a flat surface, without too much restriction from clothes. A very young baby may not like the feeling of being undressed. But as soon as she feels all right without a diaper, put her on the floor on a waterproof pad or folded towel. Dress her in a T-shirt or nothing at all. Let her kick and move freely for 15 minutes or so. Babies often enjoy a vigorous kicking session when they are dry and fresh after a bath.

You can also exercise with your baby. Hold your baby on your tummy as you do curl-ups. Or put her on your lap when bottom walking. When your baby adjusts to your movement, she strengthens her own muscles.

- **Arm raises**—With your baby lying on her back, let her grasp your fingers in each hand. Raise her arms over her head, then lower again.

- **Knee bends**—Hold your baby's lower legs. Bend her knees and bring them up toward her chest. Then bring them back down, straightening her legs.

- **Sit-ups**—You can help your baby's head control with early sit-ups. Put your baby on her back along your lap. Hold her hands and slowly raise her. At first, you will have to use one hand to support her head and neck as you lower her. But as she becomes stronger, you can just lower her slowly.

- **Head raising**—To help build strength in your baby's back. Roll a towel to a thickness of about 2 inches (6cm) and place it on the floor. Lower your baby on to her front with the towel under her shoulders and her arms forward on the floor. Then talk to her to get her attention so she lifts her head. Another approach is to lie on your back on a sofa. Place your baby on her front on top of you. Talk to her so she takes her weight on her forearms and raises her head to look at you.

- **Hip swings**—When your baby has developed some head control, hold her upright with your hands around her chest. Gently tilt her side to side in a swinging motion, so her legs swing freely. Be careful to keep her head in line with her back. Don't tilt too far so her head drops sideways.

Older babies: Your baby will still enjoy some time on the floor with little clothing. She likes to exercise.

- **Airplane**—Lie on your back with your knees to your chest. Lay your baby on her front along your shins. Hold her under her arms as you raise and lower your lower legs. Tip her back and forth or bounce her gently. You will strengthen your own abdomen and thighs. And your baby will strengthen her back and neck.

Babies are quite flexibile. Regular use of the full range of movement will help to keep them that way. As your baby becomes more active, her muscles strengthen. Stretching will keep them supple.

- **Bicycle**—With your baby on her back, hold one of her lower legs in each hand. Move her legs gently in a cycling movement. First move her as if cycling forward, then as if cycling backward.

- **Toes to nose**—Clasp your baby's calves with each hand. Gently bring one foot up toward her nose while the other leg lifts off the floor. Then lower the first leg and repeat with the other.

- **Seesaw**—A form of sit-ups. Lie on your back with feet on the floor and your knees bent. Sit your baby on your stomach and hold her hands. Begin to seesaw by curling your head and shoulders off the floor. Lean your baby back on your knees as you come up and pull her forward as you go down.

- **Wheelbarrow**—When your baby has good arm strength and can take some of her weight on her arms, place her on her front. Lift her bottom and legs as you hold her lower body. She may be able to take a step or two with her hands.

BABY MASSAGE

Another fun thing to do with your baby is massage. If you massage your baby frequently, he will enjoy it as a quiet, relaxing time. A backrub can become a way to calm and settle him down right through childhood. It is best for your baby to be naked. After a bath or while changing clothes are good times. A warm, quiet room, with soft music and dim light, will set the right mood.

You can learn certain techniques for massaging babies. But you can also see for yourself what your baby likes. Just stroke your baby and do what feels best to you. Hold your baby across your lap or on the floor. Massage with bare hands or use a little vegetable oil so the strokes glide smoothly. Be sure your hands are warm. If you use oil, warm it on your hands first. Use light, steady pressure at first. Increase it as you learn what your baby enjoys. Each movement should be slow. Repeat each one a few times.

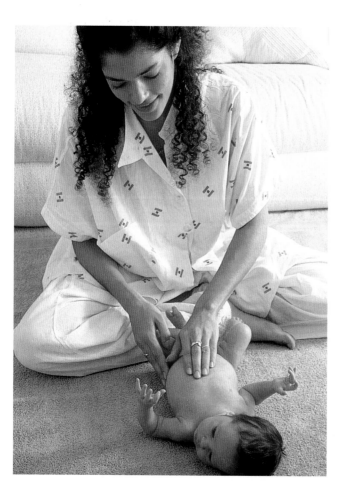

Massage techniques

Abdomen: Massage in large circles with both hands. Stroke down the center of your baby's belly and up around the sides.

Back: Stroke with both hands down the center of his back and then up the sides. Circle with your thumbs between his shoulder blades. Use your palm to rub in a circle around the small of his back.

Legs: Stroke down the back of his legs. Then lightly stroke from the top of his back down his legs. Circle up the inside of the lower leg, then back down along the outside.

Arms: Stroke down the outer arm. Then stroke very gently up the inner arm to the elbow.

QUESTIONS AND ANSWERS

Q: How old should my baby be before I can take her swimming?
A: Once she has been immunized, you can take your baby to a public swimming pool. The air and water should both be warm. But even so, your baby may get cold fairly quickly. So the swimming session should be short. Introduce her to the water by holding her with the water around you. When she is relaxed, you can let her float on her back in the water as you support her. Babies who are introduced to swimming early often feel at home in water. They don't have to overcome fear later.

Q: At eight months, my baby hardly sleeps during the day. I spend all my time trying to entertain him. How can I do my chores and make sure he doesn't get bored?
A: Include him in household jobs. Seat him near you. Give him something to play with and talk to him while you work. When you have a job to do, plan ahead to create some time when he'll be busy. Settle him nearby with something you know he enjoys. Put on a tape of music or nursery rhymes. He might like to sit in a big cardboard box with a toy. While you work, show interest in what he is doing. Talk to him from time to time. Keep watching and give him something else to do before he gets restless.

Q: Our living room looks like a bomb went off after Jane, 15 months, has been playing. Should we try to keep it tidy or let it go?
A: Too much clutter gets in the way of good play. Jane will focus better when the room is neater. It can also be a safety hazard when the floor is full of toys. Jane can learn now that things belong in their own place. You can begin to let her know it's her job to put them there. You could keep a toy box in the living room. Now and then offer to help her put toys away. She will enjoy doing it with you.

Q: I would like to be creative and save money on toys by making them myself. But because they haven't been checked for safety, will it be OK to give them to my baby?
A: You do need to be careful about homemade toys. But they are sometimes the best of all. Just use common sense. Make sure there are no small parts or bits of fluff that could come off. There should also be no sharp edges, splinters or corners. And watch out in case something falls apart and becomes dangerous.

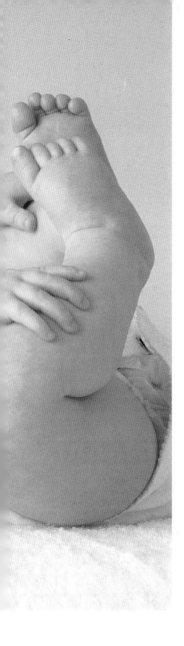

13

Healthcare

" *One night Josie woke up screaming. She felt very hot. She kept holding her hands on top of her head. I tried to settle her down, but she just kept crying. Finally I called the doctor. He met us at the emergency room in the middle of the night. He told me that I'd been right to call. He said her tonsils were infected, which can cause a bad headache. And he gave us some antibiotics to start right away. It's so hard to know what's wrong when they're too little to tell you.* "

YOUR ROLE AS A PARENT

Healthcare providers are expert helpers in guarding your baby's health. But your care is the key. You are watching over his health when you feed him, change a diaper, settle him to sleep or put a gate on the stairs.

Being healthy does not mean just being free from illness. A healthy baby will sometimes have a tummy bug or catch a cold. But a healthy baby will not fall prey to every germ that comes his way. He will be able to throw off an illness and bounce back quickly. You help your baby build up a healthy resistance to disease when you make sure he has a good diet, enough rest, exercise and doesn't get too hot or too cold.

You also protect your baby from the sources of ill health. A clean house and good hygiene with bottle-feeding or preparing baby food limits his exposure to germs. And you protect him from accidents. You childproof your house and keep an eye on safety in all his play.

You may deal with a minor health problem, such as diaper rash, yourself. You also notice when something more serious is wrong and decide when to call the doctor. When your baby's ill, you take on the role of nurse, with your doctor's help and advice.

PROFESSIONAL HEALTHCARE

A pediatrician will give your baby a complete exam before she leaves the hospital or birthing center. The same doctor will likely examine your baby again at the two-week checkup. You can call the doctor's office or clinic with any questions or concerns you may have. When you call at night, your doctor or clinic will likely have a paging system that can reach a doctor on call with whom you can speak.

You can also contact a family doctor if your baby seems ill. She may give you advice or ask you to bring him to the office. A family doctor may give your baby his vaccinations and regular checkups. He will contact a specialist if required.

Well-baby clinic

Well-baby clinics are set up to help keep babies healthy. They may be held in your doctor's office, or in a local clinic or Health Department building. Your doctor should be able to tell you where the nearest well-baby clinic is held. Or call your county Health Department in the United States. In Canada, contact your provincial or territorial Ministry of Health (see Appendix).

The well-baby clinic gives you the chance to seek advice from healthcare providers. While your baby is young, he will be weighed at each visit. The clinic may offer checkups to keep track of your baby's growth and progress. Or they may also be performed by your own doctor. Vaccines may be given at the clinic or through your doctor.

Many parents find the well-baby clinic is a place to meet other parents and babies. Some clinics organize mother-baby groups. It can help to have a chance to talk things over with others and make new friends. With a young baby, or if you have specific worries, you might want to make frequent visits to the baby clinic. Later on you might prefer to go just for vaccinations or regular check-ups. Clinics are there for you to use in the way that suits you best.

" We used to worry about germs and sterilized everything he touched. But after a while, we became more relaxed. If he dropped something, we'd just give it a quick wash and hand it back. He's got to get used to household germs. Once a baby starts moving, you can't worry about everything being 100% clean. " SONJA

VACCINATIONS

Vaccines can protect your baby from a number of serious diseases. A vaccine contains a tiny dose of an organism, which gets your baby's immune system to produce antibodies against it. These stay in his bloodstream as a defense against the organism in the future.

Vaccinations are given by injection or by mouth. They contain either a live but inactive organism, or an organism that has been killed. The organism is one that would cause the disease or a similar one. Some vaccinations require only one dose to give long-term protection. Others, such as polio, must be given in a series. Some require boosters in later years to keep working.

At a well-baby clinic, your healthcare provider can show you where your baby's weight and height fall on the range of normal growth patterns. Your baby's gains are not likely to be steady. It doesn't matter if he is large or small compared to other babies. His progress should just show regular growth.

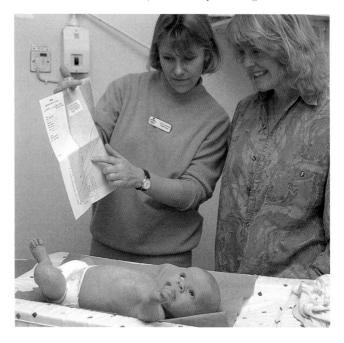

Vaccination schedules may vary. The following schedule is used in the United States.

The DPT vaccine and the type-b flu vaccine (HbCV) are given at two months, four months and six months of age. DPT combines vaccines for diptheria, tetanus and pertusis (whooping cough). A polio vaccine will also be given, most often as mouth drops, at two months and four months. The MMR vaccine is given for the first time at about 15 months. MMR combines vaccines for measles, mumps and rubella (German measles). The polio vaccine, the DPT and type-b flu vaccine are given again at about 15 months. (This completes the vaccination schedule for your baby.) Boosters will be needed at age four or five years. Your doctor or clinic will give you a booklet or card on which to record your baby's vaccinations. You can use it to keep up to date and refer to in the future.

When not to vaccinate

Your doctor may delay giving a vaccine if your baby has diarrhea, vomiting or a fever. A cold with a runny nose or cough is not a reason to delay a vaccination in most cases. Tell your doctor about any symptoms your baby may have. He will tell you if it affects the timing of vaccinations.

Some babies should not receive vaccinations because of greater risks of serious reactions. If a baby has had a severe reaction to a vaccination before, do not have it repeated. Tell your doctor if your baby suffered any damage to the nervous system at birth. Tell your doctor, too, if your baby is not developing well, has had seizures or has any known allergies. Your doctor might want to consult with a specialist before advising you further about vaccination. The whooping-cough portion of the DPT vaccine may cause a high fever or other problems.

Reactions

Parents sometimes worry about giving their baby vaccinations for fear of reactions. It is true that no vaccine can be guaranteed to be 100% without harmful effects. But it is a matter of weighing the risks against the benefits. Most vaccines are extremely safe. All are judged to provide protection that outweighs the risk of permanent harm. The diseases prevented by vaccination are not mild. They can cause death and permanent disability. The risks from the diseases are far greater than the very slight risks from the vaccines. And unless most children

I was very concerned about giving Jessica the vaccinations. I needed a lot of convincing because I had worked with children damaged by the vaccine. My wife was sure we should go ahead. I was convinced after I spoke with our doctor. He explained about the social need to prevent epidemics. It seemed selfish then not to go ahead. She was cranky for about three weeks after the MMR, but didn't have any reaction with the others. MIKE

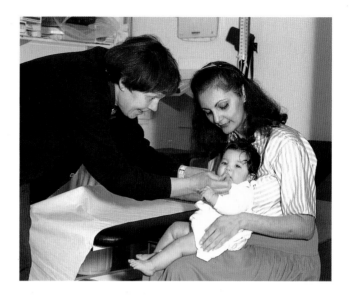

Simple drops by mouth of the polio vaccine protect children from polio. Polio used to cripple children in epidemics before the vaccine was developed. Even though polio is now rare, vaccinations must be kept up. Otherwise polio could once again sweep through a community.

are immunized against a disease, it can sweep through a community. Rarely, a child can still get a disease after being vaccinated against it. But it is almost always a milder case.

After a vaccination, you may notice no reaction at all in your baby. It is common, though, for a baby to be restless and feverish a few hours later. Less often, a baby may scream and develop a red swelling around the site of the injection. This is not a reaction that you need be too concerned about. Just try to make your baby feel better. You might try giving a dose of aceta-minophen (Tylenol®) and a cool drink of water. Sponge his arms and legs with lukewarm water if he has a fever. Contact your doctor if you are worried or if fever and crying last more than 24 hours. Rarely will a baby have a more serious reaction. If your baby shows any of these signs after vaccination, you should contact your doctor right away and take your baby to the hospital:

- high-pitched scream
- seizures
- limpness
- loss of consciousness
- pale or blue skin

Do not repeat the vaccine if your baby has had any of these reactions.

IS MY BABY ILL?

You know your baby so well that you will notice small changes that might mean your baby is ill. Her behavior can be the first clue. She may be cranky. She may wake up and cry more often. Or she may be extra sleepy, take little interest in things around her, not seem hungry or whimper.

If you suspect your baby may be ill, call a doctor. A baby's body is small. A baby has few reserves of energy and body fluids. So an illness can develop quickly and have serious effects more rapidly than it would in an older person.

177

Calling the doctor

If your baby seems ill or shows any signs of illness, call your doctor right away. Doctors know that illness can take hold quickly in babies. It's better if you call them early rather than later when it may have become more serious. Often all you need is advice over the telephone. You will be encouraged to call back if your baby doesn't get better quickly.

Illness often causes most worry at night. It can be hard to know whether to phone for advice at night or wait until morning. The chart below provides guidance about what can wait and when you should call no matter what time it is. Your doctor may have a telephone relay system at night to divert calls to a doctor on duty. So don't hang up—wait for a reply.

Be prepared to describe the signs you have noticed in your baby to your doctor. Tell him when it first started, whether she seems to be getting worse and anything you have already done for her.

NURSING YOUR ILL BABY

When your baby is ill, she doesn't know why she feels so bad. Parents can feel helpless in the face of an illness that is taking its course. But you are far from

WHEN TO CONTACT THE DOCTOR

Contact your doctor right away if your baby:
- *Is unconscious, or semi-conscious and difficult to rouse*
- *Has a convulsion*
- *Cries in pain and won't be comforted*
- *Is floppy*
- *Has trouble breathing, with either rapid or forced breaths*
- *Goes blue or very pale*
- *Vomits again and again for more than an hour*
- *Has a very weak cry or piercing high-pitched cry*
- *Has a fontanelle (soft spot on the head) that bulges or is sunken*
- *Has a dry mouth or sunken eyes*

Contact your doctor within a day if your baby:
- *Shows a marked change in behavior—is cranky, sad or listless*
- *Has vomiting and/or diarrhea that is still present after six hours*
- *Has a high fever, 100-102F (38-39C); feels hot and sweaty*
- *Won't nurse or eat*
- *Develops a rash that you can't account for*
- *Has a cough or cold if under six months*
- *Has a cough together with wheezing, barking or vomiting*
- *Has lumps (swollen glands) in the neck, armpits or groin*

helpless. Your baby may need medical care. But your tender loving care is still the best thing to help your baby through a tough time. She relies on you for courage. She trusts everything will be all right. And she finds what peace she can in the midst of her illness.

If your baby has to go into the hospital, you can stay with her. Your presence makes her feel more secure. And you can manage most of her routine care. She should be in a ward designed just for babies and children, with provision for parents. Most hospitals encourage a parent to stay overnight. But even if that is not the case, you do have a right to do so. Talk to the nursing supervisor and your doctor if you are not happy with the hospital.

" From the age of nine months, Ryan lived on antibiotics. He had ear infections constantly. I could tell right away because he'd get cranky and shake his head. It only stopped when he had tubes put in his ears when he was just two. Now I wish I'd looked into whether it was an allergic reaction that was causing the congestion in his ears. " JANE

When caring for your baby at home, take your lead from her. Don't worry if she doesn't want to eat much. She'll make up for it when she's better. She may want to be held much of the time. Or she may find the physical contact tiring and prefer lying down on her own. She may want to play. But she'll need more attention than usual.

Sickness and diarrhea

A little sickness or diarrhea is quite common. It doesn't often last long, so you can care for your baby yourself. Try to keep her on clear fluids (including very diluted fruit juice) or breast milk only until the vomiting or diarrhea stops. Then, if bottle-feeding, dilute her milk to no more than half-strength at first. If breast-feeding, try removing from your diet any cow's-milk product, including yogurt and butter. Highly spiced foods, onions, peppers and cabbage also cause problems for some breast-fed babies. Consult your doctor if your baby is not better in six hours. He may prescribe a drink to prevent dehydration.

See your doctor if your baby shows signs of projectile vomiting, where the milk is forcefully vomited across the room. In a baby between about two and six weeks, this may be a sign of *pyloric stenosis*, an obstruction of the valve outlet of the stomach. This could require surgical repair.

Fever

If your baby has a fever, feels burning hot to the touch and shivers or shakes, try to cool him down. Use only lightweight clothing and bedcovers. Keep the room nicely warm but not hot. Give extra drinks. And try a dose of acetaminophen (Tylenol®) syrup. Sponge his arms and legs with lukewarm water, or put him in a lukewarm bath.

When a baby's temperature goes very high, he may have a seizure. This can be frightening to witness. But the baby will come out of it on his own and

FIRST AID

Artificial respiration

◆ *If your baby stops breathing, send someone for medical help if you can.*

◆ *Lay your baby on his back. Tilt his head back by lifting his chin while you hold his forehead down.*

◆ *Put your mouth over his mouth and nose. Use a shallow breath, just enough to make his chest rise slightly, as you breathe out into his lungs.*

◆ *Remove your mouth to allow his chest to relax as you take a fresh breath.*

◆ *Continue until he breathes on his own or help arrives.*

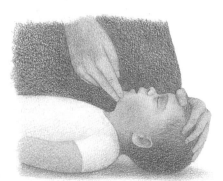 

Burns

◆ *For serious burns, cover with a sterile dressing and get medical help right away.*

◆ *For minor burns and scalds, use cold water only—no ointments or creams.*

◆ *With scalds, remove any hot, wet clothing unless it is stuck to the skin.*

◆ *Hold burned area under cold running water for up to 10 minutes.*

Scrapes and cuts

◆ *Clean scrapes with water. Wipe away from the wound. Leave uncovered to heal.*

◆ *Press a clean cloth onto a cut to stop bleeding. If anything is in the cut, press around it rather than on it.*

◆ *Wash with warm water. Dry and apply a dressing.*

◆ *If bleeding does not stop easily or a cut looks serious, seek medical aid.*

Poisoning

◆ *Try to find out what your child has taken and how much.*

◆ *Take the container or substance with you and take your baby to the doctor or emergency room of a hospital.*

◆ *Do not try to make your child vomit. This can cause more harm.*

Choking

◆ See if you can hook the object back out of her mouth with your finger. If it doesn't come right away, don't keep trying. You could push it further in.

◆ Hold your child upside down: for a **small baby**, hold her as shown below, left; for an **older baby**, sit down and lean her over your knees with the upper part of her body hanging down (see below, right).

◆ Pat firmly between her shoulder blades to loosen the object so she can cough it up.

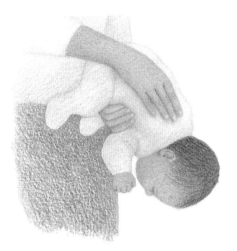
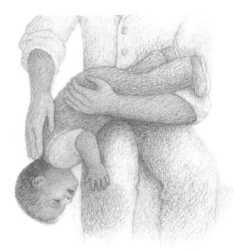

Electric shock

◆ Switch off the power.

◆ Don't use direct contact to pull your baby away from the electric source. He may be "live." Push him away from it with something that doesn't conduct electricity, such as a broom or seat cushion.

◆ Check that he is breathing. If not, give artificial respiration.

◆ Call your doctor.

Recovery position

◆ If your child is unconscious but breathing, or very drowsy after an accident, place him in the recovery position while you wait for medical help.

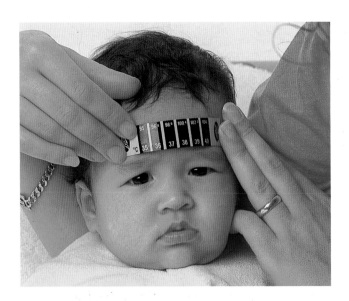

A fever strip is a quick way to learn if your baby has a fever or a temperature lower than normal. A baby's temperature can go up or down quickly. But it is a good piece of information to give your doctor if your baby seems hot and looks ill.

recover completely. Stay with him. Lay him on his side and be sure nothing is against his nose and mouth to block his breathing. When the seizure has finished, he will be drowsy or fall deep asleep. Ask someone to call the doctor when the seizure starts. Or call yourself afterward if you are alone.

Coughs and colds

Give your baby plenty of drinks. But dilute fruit juice with at least as much water as juice. Provide extra moisture in the air with a water vaporizer or a boiling a kettle in his room. Stay with it, and be sure it is out of reach if your baby is mobile. Don't use cough medicines unless prescribed by your doctor. See your doctor if a cold gets worse after the first few days. This can mean your baby has a bacterial infection.

PREVENT ACCIDENTS

It's a rare baby who never has any sort of accident. The world around us, other people and babies themselves are not always predictable. Most accidents are small things, such as something falling on a baby. Or a newly sitting baby can topple backward to bump her head.

Protecting your baby is one of your most important jobs as a parent. The risk of serious accident must always be borne in mind. Major accidents to babies do occur with tragic frequency. You can't remove all risks. But most serious accidents can be prevented with proper care.

Go through your home room by room. Check for possible hazards. These include things that are dangerous for you as well as for a crawling or toddling baby. Look for loose rugs or clutter on the floor that could trip you. If you were carrying your baby, you could both go down. Or you could drop or spill something on her.

Think ahead of your baby's development. Babyproof your home to be ready for what she may be able to do next. She may learn to climb up to an open window or open a screw-top jar before you have realized she could. Waiting until you see what she can do may be too late.

Be sure all equipment for your baby is safe. All new equipment should meet safety standards and have a clear mark of approval. Babies don't often wear out equipment. They grow and change too fast. Handed-down equipment and toys can save money and offer your baby a bigger range of activity. But check to see that secondhand equipment is in good condition. There should be no loose parts, cracks or worn joints. Most accidents don't happen on normal days when life flows smoothly. They happen at times of stress, such as when your baby is ill or tired. They happen when something special is going on and people are distracted. Or they happen when you are upset. At times like these, remember to stay alert to your baby's safety.

Within a safe place to play, your baby can explore with some freedom. Keep her safe by not just saying "no" to dangerous things. Tell her why so she begins to be aware of safety for herself.

The kitchen is the most dangerous room in the house. So use a playpen in the corner or a safety gate across the door. Your baby should not be underfoot when you are busy.

Poisonings

Most poisonings of small children occur in the middle of the afternoon. A small child gets hungry and needs to eat every two hours or so. If you expect him to wait until dinner, he can get too hungry. That's when he is more likely to get into a cupboard and try to feed himself. Household cleaners and other toxic items should never be stored within reach of a growing baby. But you can also prevent poisonings by giving your baby small meals every two hours or so, when he needs them.

HOME SAFETY

- *Think ahead to your baby's next stage of development. Childproof your home before there is a risk.*
- *Remove breakable objects from your baby's reach. Remember that she will soon be able to climb.*
- *Use safety gates on stairs, top and bottom.*
- *Use stable screens around open fires.*
- *Keep all dangerous or poisonous substances out of your baby's reach. Remember that she will soon be able to climb.*
- *Fit babyproof latches on cupboards containing anything breakable or dangerous.*
- *Keep items small enough to be swallowed out of reach.*
- *Use safety plugs in unused electric sockets.*
- *Don't let electric wires lie along the floor.*
- *Remove furniture with sharp corners, or use safety corners.*
- *Never leave hot things in the room with your baby.*
- *Use a spatter guard when you fry foods.*
- *Turn all pan handles toward the back of the stove.*
- *Put decals low on glass doors so your baby can see them.*
- *Don't use tablecloths that can be pulled down.*
- *Keep floors uncluttered. Fasten down rugs so they don't slip.*
- *Check all equipment for a safety mark of approval. Check old toys and equipment for hazards from wear.*
- *Strap your baby in a highchair. Be sure it won't tip in case she tries to climb in or out.*
- *Accidents are more likely when your baby is ill or tired, or there is confusion in the home. So try to keep things calm and keep a careful watch on things.*

QUESTIONS AND ANSWERS

Q: Can alternative medicines be used for babies?
A: Yes, some alternative therapies can be of help with health problems in babies. Homeopathic remedies, for instance, are nontoxic and safe. They often work quickly, too. Common remedies can be found in most health-food stores. Or contact the National Center for Homeopathy (see Appendix) for referral to a homeopath near you. Just because something is "natural" does not always mean it is safe for babies. So beware of herbal mixtures not meant for babies. Your doctor is a good first contact when your baby is ill. Then you might try other remedies for longer-term or recurring problems.

Q: How should I take my baby's temperature?
A: You don't always have to know the exact temperature. A baby's temperature can go up and down quickly. It doesn't always give a precise indication about illness. You can tell when your baby has a fever because she will feel very hot to the touch. Her eyes may look burning and shiny. A temperature that is lower than normal can also be a sign of illness. A normal temperature is 97-99.5F (36-37.5C).

A fever strip you hold on your baby's forehead (see page 182) is the simplest way to take her temperature. Or, hold a thermometer in her armpit for two minutes. Press her arm against her side to keep in her body heat.

Q: My baby has a cold. It's hard for him to nurse because he can't breathe well. What should I do?
A: Hold him in a warm, steamy room for a few minutes before a feeding. Sit with him in the bathroom for a few minutes while a hot shower runs. The room will fill with steam. If he is still too congested to nurse easily, ask your doctor about nosedrops to use before a feeding to clear the airways. Don't let your baby get dehydrated by missing feedings or cutting them short while he has a cold.

Q: We have been sterilizing anything that might go in our baby's mouth, such as rattles and teething rings. When is it safe to stop sterilizing?
A: Most household germs will not make your baby ill. In fact, she was born with some immunities to the germs that are around you all the time. The more-dangerous germs are in warm, damp places and in food. That's why it's important to sterilize food and feeding equipment. With other items, being clean is good enough. If a rattle is dropped on the floor, a good wash with soap and hot water will do. If you sterilize everything she touches, you will just delay your baby from building her own immunities.

APPENDIX

These groups offer information, support and referral when you are planning a pregnancy, are pregnant or have a baby. Many operate nationwide. Some are small, run by people who give what help they can. Often their services have to fit in with family demands. So please offer to phone back at a good time. Enclose a stamped, self-addressed envelope if you request information.

GENERAL INFORMATION

These groups provide general information and services. They can also put you in touch with the right group for your needs.

American College of Obstetricians and Gynecologists, Resource Center, 409 12th Street, S.W., P.O. Box 96920 Washington, D.C. 20090-6920. Write for information about pregnancy, labor, birth or postpartum issues. Send a separate self-addressed stamped envelope for each topic about which you need information.

March of Dimes Birth Defects Foundation, 1275 Mamaroneck Ave., White Plains, New York 10605. Call: 1-888-MODIMES between 9 a.m. and 5 p.m. Eastern Standard Time. Or call: 914-428-7100. TTY: 914-997-4763 URL: http://www.modimes.org E-mail: resourcecenter@modimes. Regional offices throughout the United States. Operates a toll-free Resource Center, which provides information and referral. Issues addressed include pregnancy, pre-pregnancy, birth defects, genetics, drug use and toxic hazards during pregnancy, or related topics.

The Women's Bureau Publications (United States). United States Department of Labor, Women's Bureau Clearing House, Box EX, 200 Constitution Ave., N.W., Washington, D.C. 20210. Call toll-free 1-800-827-5335. Information about state laws on family leave.

CONCEPTION, PREGNANCY AND CHILDBIRTH

American Academy of Husband-Coached Childbirth (Bradley Method), P.O. Box 5224, Sherman Oaks, CA 91413. Call 1-800-423-2397, or 818-788-6662. Childbirth-educator training and referral to Bradley Method childbirth educators.

American Cancer Society (Help quitting smoking.) Call toll-free: 1-800-227-2345.

American College of Nurse-Midwives (ACNM), 818 Connecticut Avenue N.W., Suite 900, Washington, D.C. 20006. Call: 202-728-9860. Information and referral.

American Society for Psychoprophylaxis in Obstetrics (ASPO/Lamaze), 1200 19th Street N.W., Suite 300, Washington, D.C. 20036-2422. Call toll-free: 1-800-368-4404. Childbirth-educator training and referral to ASPO/Lamaze childbirth educators.

Association of Labor Assistants and Childbirth Educators (ALACE) P.O. Box 382724, Cambridge, MA 02238-2724. Call: 617-441-2500. Trains and certifies labor assistants and birth educators. Provides information and referral.

Doulas of North America, 1100 23rd Avenue East, Seattle, WA 98112. Fax: 206-325-0472. Doulas provide prenatal, childbirth and postpartum in-home support.

Informed Homebirth. Call: 313-662-6857. Information regarding homebirth.

International Cesarean Awareness Network (ICAN), 1304 Kingsdale Avenue, Redondo Beach, CA 90278. Call: 310-542-6400

International Childbirth Education Association, P.O. Box 20048, Minneapolis, MN 55420-0048. Call: 612-854-8660

Midwives Alliance of North America (MANA), P.O. Box 175, Newton, KS 67114. Call: 316-283-4543

National Association of Childbearing Centers (NACC), 3123 Gottschall Road, Perkiomenville, PA 18074. Call: 215-234-8068. Referral to birthing centers throughout the United States.

Planned Parenthood. Call toll-free: 1-800-230-PLAN. Information, referral, and clinical services. Care includes fertility, birth control, sexual health and prenatal care. Fees for all clinical services, including prenatal care, are based on a sliding scale according to ability to pay.

Public Citizen's Health Research Group, 1600 20th Street N.W., Washington, D.C. 20009. Call: 202-588-1000. Information about C-sections, vaginal births after Cesarean section (VBACs), and other pregnancy and birth-related concerns.

WIC Program (Supplemental Feeding Program for Women, Infants and Children). Provides nutrition education and support and free food coupons. Serves low-income pregnant women, breast-feeding mothers and children with poor nutrition to age five. In the United States, call your state or local Department of Public Health.

AFTER THE BIRTH

American Academy of Pediatrics, 141 Northwest Point Blvd., Elk Grove Village, IL. Call: 847-228-5005; fax: 847-228-5097

Child Help. Call toll-free: 1-800-4A-CHILD (1-800-422-4453). National child abuse hot-line for parents in crisis or children at risk.

Danny Foundation, 3158 Danville Blvd., P.O. Box 680, Alamo, CA 94507. Call toll-free: 1-800-83-DANNY. Provides information on crib safety.

Depression After Delivery, P.O. Box 1282, Morrisville, PA 19067. Call toll-free: 1-800-944-4773

INFACT Canada, 10 Trinity Square, Toronto, M5G 1B1 Canada. Call: 416-595-9819; fax: 416-591-9355; e-mail: infact@ftn.net Provides breast-feeding information, support, and referral.

International Lactation Consultant Association (ILCA), 200 North Michigan Ave., Suite 300, Chicago, IL 60601-3821. Call: 312-541-1710; fax: 312-541-1271

La Leche League Canada, 18C Industrial Drive, P.O. Box 29, Chesterville, Ontario K0C 1H0 Canada. Call: 613-448-1842; fax: 613-448-1845

La Leche League Canada Français, Secretariat General de la LLL, C.P. 874 Ville St. Laurent, Quebec H4L 4W3 Canada. Call: 514-747-9127; fax: 514-747-6667

La Leche League International, 1400 North Meacham Road, Schaumburg, IL 60173. Call toll-free: 1-800-LA-LECHE, or 847-519-7730; fax: 847-519-0035. Call 1-900-448-7475, ext. 55 for recorded advice (toll call). La Leche League's website is: http//www.laleche-league.org/.

Medela, Inc., P.O. Box 660, McHenry, IL 60051. Call toll-free: 1-800-TELL-YOU. Provides information and referral regarding breast pumps, related products and breast-feeding specialists.

Safety Belt Safe USA, 123 Manchester Blvd., Inglewood, CA 90301. Call: 310-673-2666. Information regarding safety and correct installation of car seats and safety belts.

Wellstart, 4062 First Avenue, San Diego, CA 92130. Call: 619-295-5192. Breast-feeding information.

SINGLE PARENTS

National Organization of Single Mothers, P.O. Box 68, Midland, NC 28107-0068. Call: 704-888-KIDS

MULTIPLE BIRTHS

Mothers of Supertwins (MOST), P.O. Box 951, Brentwood, NY 11717. Call: 516-434-MOST. Provides information, support and referral for parents of triplets or more.

Mothers of Twins Clubs, Inc., P.O. Box 23188, Albuquerque, NM 87192-1188. Call: 505-275-0955

Triplet Connection, P.O. Box 99571, Stockton, CA 95209. Call: 209-474-0885

Twin-to-Twin Transfusion Syndrome (TTTS) Foundation, 411 Longbeach Parkway, Bay Village, OH 44140. Call: 216-899-8887

Twin Services, P.O. Box 10066, Berkeley, CA 94709. Call: 510-524-0863

Twins Magazine, 5350 S. Roslyn Street, Suite 400, Englewood, CO 80111. Call toll-free: 1-800-328-3211

BEREAVEMENT

Center for Loss in Multiple Birth, c/o Jean Kollantai, P.O. Box 1064, Palmer, AK 99645. Call: 907-746-6123

SPECIAL NEEDS

Allergy and Asthma Network, 3554 Chain Bridge Road, Suite 200, Fairfax, VA 22030. Call toll-free: 1-800-878-4403

American Cleft Palate Foundation, 1218 Grandview Avenue, Pittsburgh, PA 15211. Call toll-free: 1-800-24-CLEFT, or call: 412-481-1376

About Face U.S.A. (Information and support for parents of a child with a cleft palate or other facial abnormality.) Call toll-free: 1-800-225-FACE.

About Face Canada. Call toll-free: 1-800-665-FACE. International office. Information and support for parents of a child with a cleft palate or other facial abnormality.

CARESS, P.O. Box 1492, Washington, D.C. 20013. Information for parents of children with disabilities.

Direct Link for the Disabled, Inc., P.O. Box 1036, Solvang, CA 93464. Call: 805-688-1603; fax: 805-686-5285 or 805-686-5284; e-mail: suharry@terminus.com Has a large computerized network of 14,000 local, state and national resources. Rare disorders, complicated situations and denial of benefits are specialties.

ECMO Moms and Dads, c/o Blair and Gayle Wilson, P.O. Box 53848, Lubbock, TX 79453. Call: 806-794-0259. Information for parents of premature infants.

Friends' Health Connection, P.O. Box 114, New Brunswick, NJ 08903. Call toll-free: 1-800-48-FRIEND or 908-418-1811; fax: 908-249-9897; website: http://www. 48friend. com; e-mail: fhc@pilot.njin.net Custom support for persons and their families with health-related problems. Connects people who have the same health problems on a one-to-one basis so they can communicate for friendship and support.

Intensive-care Parenting, ICU Parenting Magazine, RD #10, Box 176, Brush Creek Road, Irwin, PA 15642

National Association of Postpartum Care Services, 8910 229th Place, SW, Edmonds, WA 98020. Referral to a certified postpartum doula.

National Organization for Rare Disorders (NORD), P.O. Box 8923, New Fairfield, CT 06812

National Down Syndrome Society (NDSS), 666 Broadway, New York, NY 10012-2317. Call toll-free: 1-800-221-4602

National Information Center for Children and Youth with Disabilities, P.O. Box 1492, Washington, D.C. 20013-1492. Call toll-free: 1-800-695-0285

National Reye's Syndrome Foundation, 426 N. Lewis Street, Bryan, OH 43506. Call toll-free: 1-800-233-7393. In Ohio, call: 1-800-231-7393

Sidelines, a nonprofit organization for women with a complicated pregnancy. Puts women in touch with volunteers who have been through a similar experience. Call Candace Hurley, executive director: 714-497-2265, or Tracy Hoogenboom: 909-563-6199.

CANADIAN PROVINCIAL OR TERRITORIAL MINISTRIES OF HEALTH

Alberta, Alberta Health, 24th Floor, 10025 Jasper Ave., Edmonton, AB T5J 2P. Call: 403-427-2653; fax: 403-427-2511

British Columbia, Prevention and Health Promotion Branch, Ministry of Health, Main Floor, 1520 Blanshard St., Victoria, BC V8W 3C8. Call: 604-952-1531; fax: 604-952-1570

Manitoba, Manitoba Health, 599 Empress St., Room 259, 2nd Floor, Box 925, Winnipeg, Manitoba R3C 2T6. Call: 204-786-7305; fax: 204-772-2943

New Brunswick, Department of Health and Community Services, P.O. Box 5100, Fredericton, New Brunswick, E3B 5G8. Call: 506-453-2933; fax: 506-453-2726

Newfoundland, Community Health, Department of Health, Confederation Bldg., West Block, P.O. Box 8700, St. John's, NF A1B 4J4. Call: 709-729-3110; fax: 709-729-5824

Northwest Territories, Child/Family Support Division, Department of Health and Social Services, Government of the Northwest Territories, 5th Floor Precambrian Bldg. 6, P.O. Box 1320, Yellowknife, NWT X1A 2L9. Call: 403-873-7054; fax: 403-873-7706

Nova Scotia, Health Promotion Division, Nova Scotia Department of Health, 1690 Hollis St., 11th Floor, P.O. Box 488, Halifax, NS B3J 2R8. Call: 902-424-5011; fax: 902-424-0558

Ontario, Ministry of Health, 5700 Yonge Street, 5th Floor, Toronto, Ontario M2M 4K5. Call: 416-314-5485; fax: 416-314-5497

Prince Edward Island, Health and Community Services Agency, 4 Sydney St., P.O. Box 2000, Charlottetown, PEI, C1A 7N8. Call: 902-368-6522; fax: 902-368-6136

Quebec, Federation des Centres locales de sante communautair, 1801, de Maison-neuve ouest, Piece 600, Montreal, Quebec H3H 1J9. Call: 514-931-1448; fax: 514-931-9577

Saskatchewan, Population Health Branch, Saskatchewan Health, 3475 Albert St., Regina, SK S4S 6X6. Call: 306-787-7113 or 787-7110; fax: 306-787-7095

Yukon, Whitehorse Regional Hospital, #5 Hospital Road, Whitehorse, Yukon Y1A 3H7. Call: 403-667-8700, fax: 403-667-8778

INDEX